THE DYING CHILD

Second Edition

THE DYING CHILD

The Management of the
Child or Adolescent Who is Dying

By

WILLIAM M. EASSON, M.D.

Professor and Head
Department of Psychiatry and Behavioral Sciences
Louisiana State University Medical Center
New Orleans, Louisiana

CHARLES C THOMAS • PUBLISHER

Springfield • Illinois • U.S.A.

Published and Distributed Throughout the World by

CHARLES C THOMAS • PUBLISHER
Bannerstone House
301-327 East Lawrence Avenue, Springfield, Illinois, U.S.A.

© *1970 and 1981, by* CHARLES C THOMAS • PUBLISHER
ISBN 0-398-04075-3
First Edition, First Printing, 1970
First Edition, Second Printing, 1972
First Edition, Third Printing, 1977
Second Edition, 1981

Library of Congress Catalog Card Number: 80-22664

*With THOMAS BOOKS careful attention is given to all details of
manufacturing and design. It is the Publisher's desire to present books that are
satisfactory as to their physical qualities and artistic possibilities and
appropriate for their particular use. THOMAS BOOKS will be true to those
laws of quality that assure a good name and good will.*

Easson, William M   1931-
    The dying child.

    Bibliography: p.
    Includes index.
    1. Terminally ill children.   I. Title.
RJ249.E27   1981   362.1'98920029   80-22664
ISBN 0-398-04075-3

Printed in the United States of America
PS-RX-1

PREFACE TO THE SECOND EDITION

While a great deal has been written about death and dying in the last decade, there has been little direct investigation as to how people of any age understand the meaning of their own death or how they cope with their own dying. Clinicians, family members and those who work with the dying need to keep in mind that much of what is presently published about death and dying is theoretical, sometimes overgeneralized and frequently applicable only to limited situations, to patients with certain levels of maturity or personality style and to specific social and cultural environments.

In dealing with children and adolescents who are dying, the needs of the young patient should always dictate the management. People adapt to dying with the understanding and the strengths appropriate to their age, and on this basis they should be helped.

In preparing this new edition, I am most grateful to Mrs. Marilyn Peak and Mrs. Constance Deck for their consistently efficient help and support.

W.M.E.

PREFACE TO THE FIRST EDITION

This book is repetitious and incomplete—and it could not be otherwise.

As the growing child learns the meaning of personal death this knowledge stays with him for the rest of his life. He cannot escape what he now understands. What he comprehends as an infant, he has to deal with as a student, a parent and a grandparent. With each stage in his development, he has to adapt to what he has known before and what he now learns. Since this book outlines the preadult phases of human growth, it must show how the knowledge of death is handled at each developmental level and will again have to be coped with at a stage of further growth— repetitious, unavoidable, until death itself gives the final knowledge.

At this stage of human evolution, the concept of death is still beyond man's total understanding. Poets and preachers, teachers and soldiers, the wise and the foolish—mankind ponders the meaning of death but still does not completely know. This book deals with the practical day-to-day realities of dying and with the management of predictable problems. It cannot answer the unanswerable where even the question is not clear.

The author is especially grateful to Miss Sandra Spillis, who carried the major burden of preparation of this manuscript.

W.M.E.

CONTENTS

THE DYING CHILD

Chapter One

THE CHILD'S UNDERSTANDING

OF DEATH

A child copes with his own dying with the intellectual understanding and the emotional strengths of a child. Children handle their dying in ways that are natural to their age level. They can deal with their own approaching death only as they understand the meaning of dying and in the fashion that is appropriate to their level of maturity.

Like any other life experience, the manner in which death is faced depends on the emotional capabilities of the person who is living through this life happening. The adult grapples with the work of dying with the strength and the capabilities of the experienced man or woman. The aged react to death, this final growth task, with the intellectual appreciation and the emotional responses of those who have lived long and seen much. When it is a child or an adolescent who has to live through this very personal experience of dying, the young person faces a task that he can understand only at the level of a child or adolescent and that he can handle only with the personal strengths available to a young child or a teenager. The child always lives and dies as a child.

Across the world, the patterns of dying in childhood are being modified in response to the advances in medicine and public health and to the changing pace of society. In the developing nations, infectious diseases and perinatal trauma are still the most frequent causes of death in childhood, but in the industrialized countries, childhood death is most often due to accidents and acute trauma. The young boys, playing with matches, set a fire from which they cannot escape. The blithely adventurous toddler explores his way out the kitchen door and falls down the stairs to his death. The energetic schoolchild, full of life, runs happily after the ball and into the path of the automobile. The little girl who wants so much to be like her mother swallows Mommy's pills and poisons herself. In accidents such as these, a healthy, happy child is one moment alive and full of hope and the next abruptly and unexpectedly killed. The child himself has little time to react to the swift reality of his death. His family is left to face this sudden cruel loss without warning or preparation. Happy dreams give way to mourning. The family needs support in these unfortunate situations. The child is beyond help (Limerick, 1978).

Extended dying, over months or years, is now much more common in childhood than it was several decades ago. With expert medical and surgical care, a child is more likely to survive the immediate injury of an accident but linger crippled and disfigured, to die gradually over a longer time (Howard, 1961). The congenitally handicapped child, who formerly would have died at birth or in early infancy, now survives with good medical care to an older age and dies over a much longer period. The youngster with a malignant tumor is now kept alive for many more weeks or months by intensive medical procedures and by multiple surgical interventions. The leukemic child is more likely to live longer due to the transfusions and drug treatments he receives and thus takes much longer to die. The chronic nephritic youngster can be kept alive with repeated renal dialysis, and so death is delayed. A kidney transplant may further extend the life of this child and also the duration of his dying. The youngster with cystic fibrosis is more sure of surviving infancy but is still liable to die slowly over months and years due to repeated lung infections. To an increasing extent, fatally ill children live longer and die longer.

Dying used to be a family affair, but children and adults now go to hospitals to die. Most often the person who is dying has no part in deciding where he wants to die. He usually is not consulted, child or adult, and frequently would prefer to die at home if he were asked. Nowadays when a child dies at home, the death is likely to have been caused by a sudden accident. Children who take longer to die do much of their dying in a hospital, and where the management of the dying child is a problem, the youngster is usually dying slowly, in a hospital at least periodically and frequently in pain.

As the child dies, the young patient and his family may come to recognize that the medical and surgical procedures are likely to map out the manner and the time of the child's dying (Glaser and Strauss, 1965). The youngster's death can be programmed and orchestrated by the treatment he receives. The treatment itself may finally produce death (Tietz, 1975). That extra transfusion may maintain life just those few hours or days so that the leukemic child can whisper a few additional sentences, even though the child is exhausted and racked with pain. The additional dialysis may briefly restore energy to the nephritic child for a few extra days so that he can give that final, feeble smile of recognition. Hypnotic drugs give merciful relief to the child dying painfully of a malignancy so that the youngster can sleep more peacefully in the arms of his mother; the same medication may also sedate the child so much that approaching death is hastened and the final sleep comes sooner.

While there has been a much more open discussion about death and dying in recent years, much of this literature has dealt primarily with the social role of the dying adult in his culture or has focused on the reactions of the bereaved to the diagnosis and the treatment. Frequently authors do not define what exactly they are considering when they write of death. When the bibliography dealing with the dying child and the child's reaction to death is reviewed, the reader must first clarify what aspect of death is being considered and just how this is being related to children. Certain writers discuss what they describe as the child's reaction to death when really they are evaluating a healthy child's understanding of death as a general philosophical concept— death as opposed to life, an abstract, impersonal idea, something that happens to other people. It is very different when a person contemplates his own death as opposed to thinking about others' dying. Very little is written about how the dying child thinks and feels about his own dying. Some authors examine the child's response to death but deal only with the response of the bereaved child to the death of another person, to the loss of a meaningful relationship. Other writers are really describing how a child copes with a fatal illness when they consider the child's reaction to death. In managing the dying child, all aspects of the youngster's death and dying must be understood. The correct treatment of the dying youngster and his family can be based only on the understanding of what his approaching death means to the child and his famiy and on an appreciation of how this young patient can reasonably be expected to cope with this life task.

A child's reaction to his own dying and death always depends on his intellectual and emotional maturity. The youngster deals with his approaching death according to the way he understands his situation, and he responds to this problem in the same fashion that he deals with other life tasks. While a child is growing and maturing, he is at the same time developing a changing understanding of what his own death means. He deals with this increasing appreciation of the meaning of death in different ways as he matures intellectually and emotionally. The child's awareness of the meaning of his personal death can be categorized in different growth stages.

TABLE I
DEVELOPMENTAL STAGES IN THE UNDERSTANDING OF
PERSONAL DEATH

Aspect of Death to Which Child Responds	*Age When Child Obviously Begins to React*
Physical reaction to dying ("death agony")	Birth
Reactions of parents, family and other people	1-2 months
Treatment procedures	1-2 months
Personal recognition of body changes due to disease and and treatment	3-4 years
Changes in individual self (me—not me)	4 years
Significance of diagnosis	4-6 years
Significance of prognosis	5-7 years
Change in relationships and social role	4-8 years

Physiological Death

With every ounce of strength, a newborn anencephalic child will fight for his next breath of life. Even though he lacks a fully developed brain, this child uses all his energy in his struggle for survival. The comatose infant, unresponsive to external stimuli, still strives with his whole being for one more breath. Automatically, and without any teaching, the drowning youngster reaches with every muscle for one extra moment of existence. From the very beginning of life, each human being has this innate physiological mechanism that reflexly strives to maintain life. This physical reaction is influenced by higher brain centers but appears to be primarily a function of more simple reflex processes.

The feeling of tension that accompanies this primitive physiological struggle for survival is, with good reason, often referred to as the "death agony"—a pervasive, nightmarish sense of deepest anxiety. Intuitively every human being seems to dread this feeling and tries to avoid, at all costs, this very disturbing physiologically based sensation (Maurer, 1961). The death agony is probably the most unpleasant physical experience to which the human being is subject, but whenever death is approaching, this inner feeling of tension grows closer and becomes more intense. The individual strives desperately to avoid this pervasive distress, no matter how old or how young he may be. Often the struggle to escape the death agony and to survive weakens the dying person even further and actually hastens death. The dying person cannot avoid some experience of the death agony, however brief, and must live through these unpleasant sensations as he passes from life to death.

Physical Changes Due to Illness and Treatment

The way a child deals with his death and dying is markedly influenced by the physical changes caused by the illness and by the reaction of the people around him to these changes. The youngster's disease may produce deformities that frighten other children so that they ridicule or reject the dying child. The youngster may become grotesque because he is thin and cadaverous, or swollen and bloated. He may develop a tumor or deformity that leaves him ugly and repulsive. Drugs that maintain the child's life may also cause his hair to fall out and his skin to become red and scaly. The child may become so disfigured by the illness or the treatment that his appearance makes his family and friends so anxious that they avoid him. Headaches, bleeding, tiredness and irritability make a youngster much more difficult to endure and leave him much less emotional energy to deal with the stresses of his illness.

Even in early infancy, the young child can sense when he is making people tense or angry. When a deformed child feels his mother's cringing when she holds him, he too becomes more anxious and frightened. From that time on, he is more hesitant to seek comfort and consolation from his mother. When the young child finds that his cries of pain do not bring relief because people who care for him are bothered that he is in pain, he then tends to become more withdrawn and more hopeless. His pleas become more plaintive, and eventually he lapses into overwhelmed apathy. Any youngster, no matter how old or how young, feels good when he is appreciated and welcomed. When a child is sick and dying and senses that he disturbs or disgusts people, he tends to think of himself as bad or unlovable. His emotional growth becomes more and more stunted, so he is less able to deal with the stresses of his illness and approaching death. From the first months of life, the dying child is responding to the reaction of those around him to his illness—to his parents and family members, to the neighbors and to the professionals who treat him. The reactions of the dying child will reflect those feelings and responses.

As a child gets older, he is more able to recognize and respond himself to the changes in his body produced by the illness and the treatment. By age three or four, the little girl has learned that reflection in the mirror is her face, her hands and her body, and she may feel bitterness and disgust as she sees her mirror reflection slowly wither over the months. The kindergarten child will come to hate himself for those purple leukemic spots he sees on his arms and his legs. The teenager is likely to despise himself for the spreading weakness he cannot combat. From the preschool years, the growing child has the ability to recognize and respond to the signs and effects of physical changes due to illness and treatment procedures. The youngster's reaction to these aspects of dying will have a major effect on his ability to cope with the task of dying.

Treatment Procedures

As the child approaches death, often he is faced with the day-to-day reality of unpleasant treatment procedures—the repeated injections, the bewildering surgery and the excruciating pain when the dressings are changed. He finds that he has no control over what happens to him, and increasingly he lives by rules set by others. The very young child cannot understand that all this is supposed to help him.

When the youngster is admitted to the hospital, the admission procedures are bewildering but are usually tolerated fairly well as long as the parents are there. However, when people try to take away the child's own clothes, then the strangeness and the uncertainty become more immediate and more frightening. The young patient realizes he is expected to sleep and even live in a strange bed, eat unfamiliar food and do what strangers tell him. Often children cannot understand verbal explanations of what is happening. The child knows only the loneliness and the misery he is experiencing, and he responds to this pain. From the first months of life, the youngster can be conditioned by repeated painful experiences, even the experiences that are expected to be therapeutic, to respond with fear and anxiety to the very people who are supposed to be caring for him—but who tend to bring him pain, pain due to the illness, pain due to the treatment.

From two or three months of age, the young child is able to remember that white coats bring more pain, and he may start to react in fear and anxiety to all people in white. Treatment personnel, nurses, physicians and aides are likely to be bothered when they find that the child patient fears them. They may become so uncomfortable that they tend to keep away from this child, even though he really needs their care and attention.

These conditioned responses to strange and painful treatment appear in early infancy and will occur in the management of any severely ill child. Once a fear response is established, it is difficult then to relieve the child's anxiety. When a young child is dying, these anxious reactions to the treatment situation and the treatment procedures may complicate his overall management. Parents, family and clinicians need to be aware of what the child faces. As far as possible they should work to minimize the strangeness, the fear and the pain and maximize the familiarity, the predictability and the security. Dying is difficult enough without treatment procedure anxieties.

Changes in the Self—Personal Death

Before the growing child can understand that his death means a change in his individual existence, he must first know that he is a separate, unique individual. The child has to have a solid appreciation that he is an individual being, a Self, "I," "myself," before he can start to appreciate that his own death will mean the difference between "me" and "not me."

As the growing infant begins to respond to people and things around him, he is learning also that he is a separate being—that there is something outside of himself, separate from his Self. When the young child starts to reach for a toy, he is learning at the same time that he exists separate from other things and from other people around him. As he begins to crawl and then to walk on his own, this sense of personal separateness and individuality becomes more definite and more personal. Gradually the toddler learns that he can wander around the corner, out of mother's sight on his own, by himself. To an increasing extent the youngster starts to assert his own opinions and thus to emphasize his difference, his uniqueness and his separateness from the world around. With each demand and each surge of negativism, the growing youngster is emphasizing himself and showing his family and himself that he is indeed a person, a Self. The child begins to talk on his own behalf and to express himself as "I." With each self-assertion, this "I" in "I want" or "I will" has a more definite personal meaning to the youngster, emphasizing over and over again that he is a person, separate and unique.

By the time that he is three or four years of age, the youngster knows with increasing certainty that he is indeed a separate physical and emotional being. While he is learning that he is indeed a "me," he is at the same time beginning to appreciate that somehow there could also be a "not me." When the growing child comes to understand, even tenuously, the reality that he exists as a unique, separate person, he also begins to question where he came from and whence he is going.

This awareness that "me" could somehow become "not me" is extremely unsettling not only to the young child but to every person from childhood onward. The appreciation that somehow a time could come when we could cease to be is deeply disturbing to each of us. The individual finds it very difficult to grasp the full significance that somehow he might stop existing. This thought is often too overwhelming and sometimes too frightening. While the physiological death agony is the most unpleasant physical sensation that man has to face, undoubtedly the awareness that an individual might cease to be is the most awesome psychological feeling a person can have about himself and his existence. To the ordinary, average person, the possibility of absolute nonbeing is very difficult to conceive and almost unthinkable. It is questionable whether any human being can really fully face or completely understand and appreciate "not being." In psychoanalytic terms, "in the unconscious, every one of us is convinced of his own immortality" (Freud, 1915). Normal people do not have adequate emotional defenses to deal constantly with such deeply disturbing self-concepts (Cappon, 1959; Stokes, 1960). All people, no matter what age they may be, deal with these dreaded and dread-producing feelings by denial, normally, naturally and in an emotionally healthy fashion. The unanswerable questions and the overwhelming meaning of a possible "not me" state (the concept that an individual may completely cease to be) is automatically covered over and hidden away emotionally because such feelings evoke too much anxiety. Though these thoughts and feelings are kept out of awareness, the anxieties they arouse are handled by normal age-appropriate defenses. The young adult may absolutely avoid considering the possibility of personal death and furiously resist or ignore anything to do with death and dying. Personal death is just not to be considered in the young adult years. The middle-aged adult shuts out the meaning and the possibility of personal dying and handles the underlying anxieties by making the concept of death an interesting intellectual exercise, a subject to be studied, a fascinating philosophical topic.

As soon as the young child begins to appreciate that he is a separate human being, he starts to understand dimly that somehow this precious individuality could cease to be. He begins to shut out this new awareness and these anxious feelings as soon as they are felt. Typically the child is four or five years of age before he has a clearly defined stable concept of himself as a separate individual. It is at about this age also that the youngster has to deal with his feelings about being and not being. Normally and naturally, these anxieties are covered over and dealt with by denial and repression, but sometimes a preschool child cannot totally repress these anxieties. This is the age when nightmares are most often seen in normal children. When the four-year-old goes to bed and lies there in the dark, he realizes that he is a small individual, all alone and separate, in a world where other people and things are so big and sometimes so menacing. The youngster is now aware that he is vulnerable, that somehow he could be overwhelmed and annihilated, that "me" could be swept into "not me." The child has now matured emotionally and intellectually to the level where he understands that he is a separate individual. He also appreciates that this separate individuality could cease to exist. With the greater emotional strength that comes with the school years, the maturing child gradually becomes more able to keep these disturbing feelings more controlled and further from awareness. The nightmares then cease, and the child sleeps peacefully.

The four-year-old, sometimes the three-year-old, and usually the five-year-old, has a definite understanding of his own individuality and his separate self. At this age then, he has the emotional and intellectual ability to be deeply upset by what he feels to be a threat to his existence. He has matured enough now that he can be disturbed, sometimes deeply upset, by an illness that seems to threaten his survival in this world. The growing youngster of this age handles any feelings that his existence is threatened primarily by denial. However, when death is growing nearer, the dying youngster will find it increasingly difficult to deny relentless reality, and more and more of his emotional strength will be used to blot out those deep fears that he might indeed be overwhelmed and destroyed. The child who is weaker physically as the disease advances finds himself weaker emotionally also and thus less able to deny the mounting threat to his existence. The energy he should be using to fight his illness and to live as long as possible, he may have to spend trying to shut out his fears of annihilation. Those nightmares of younger years may now recur because his annihilation anxiety has increased or because psychologically he has become exhausted.

The youngster can become increasingly restless as he senses the approach of death and no longer is able to deny that "me" could become "not me." The restlessness of the dying child sometimes indicates that he is less able to control his anxieties as death grows nigh and is a sign that his strength is failing. Approaching death may be heralded by increasingly unsettled behavior, by irritability and uncontrolled angry outbursts. The astute clinician will understand that this more childlike behavior is a sign that death is growing near (Beigler, 1957). The child is sensing that his individuality is coming to an end. His existence is about to cease. His denial is no longer completely effective. His inner anxieties that his Self is dying are shown outwardly by his more disturbing and disturbed behavior.

As the child is growing older and developing his individuality and self-pride, he is also becoming increasingly independent. He enjoys this feeling of mastery and self-sufficiency. Dying, however brings with it an enforced dependency, and death the absolute dependent state. The young child, newly self-sufficient, must face the loss of self-control and independence when he is fatally ill. He will resent the fact that he can no longer do what he wants to do in the way that he wishes. He is likely to be angry, very understandably angry, since he was once able to do physically what he is no longer capable of doing. The young boy can no longer play on the ball team because he bruises too easily and becomes tired too easily. The little girl cannot go cycling with her friends because her unsteadiness would make her fall. These children are ready to be active and independent, but a fatal illness and death robs them of their independence. These children find themselves more and more limited at a time in their lives when their natural tendency is to want to do things for themselves. While the child may be angry and bitter at the physical disease process, this resentment may be caused just as much by the obligatory dependency forced on him by the disease. The child's frustration and fury may rise more from his inability to assert himself and to do things for himself than from his resentment at the approach of death.

From a very young age, the growing child enjoys the feeling of mastery. He finds more and more pleasure in his Self. He will resist and resent any disease process that prevents his self-assertion and threatens his self-existence.

The Diagnosis

When the fatally ill youngster begins to recognize and understand the meaning of his diagnosis, his reaction to his illness will be greatly influenced by this knowledge. In recent years a great deal has been written about the reaction of dying people to their illness and death (Kubler-Ross, 1969). The focus of much of this literature has been on the patient's reaction to the diagnosis, the recognition that he is fatally ill. Some clinicians have accepted uncritically that all patients go through sequential stages of adaptation to a terminal illness even though the writers who propose these stages emphasize that each dying person responds in his own way. Some professionals appear to impose these sequential responses to a fatal illness on their patients in an overenthusiastic attempt to help dying patients cope in a way that the clinicians believe most meaningful. As Garfield (1978) and others have pointed out, no systematic observation has verified any preprogrammed stages, and no uniform sequence of adaptation to a terminal illness has ever been proven.

The clinician must understand that a child's response to his disease diagnosis is always a function of his intellectual growth, his emotional maturity and his life experience. The three-year-old girl can run gaily to her visiting parents, shouting as she skips to meet them, "Mommy, I've got leukemia and a new dress." The little girl has no real understanding of what this diagnosis "leukemia" means. She has no understanding of what this term should mean to her now or what this leukemia will do to her in the future. Her parents are likely to be overwhelmed at this diagnosis, but at age three, a young child will be unconcerned because people say she has "leukemia." The older she is, however, the more she will understand, and the more she will become concerned.

Social and cultural factors play a very large part in teaching the child the meaning of diagnoses. With the increasingly successful antismoking campaign across the world, children at a younger and younger age have learned from television, the radio and other news media what the words "cancer," "tuberculosis" and "emphysema" and the phrase "heart disease" mean. Television news broadcasts show world leaders who are cut down before the child's eye by some process that is given a name, a diagnosis. Day after day, on the radio and television, melodramas and "soap operas" so beloved by children and many of their parents are used as the easiest available mechanical babysitters, and from these programs, impressionable children are taught the meaning of diagnoses and diseases. The heroes and the heroines take weeks and months to waste away and die, while the diagnosis is repeated again and again for the child to learn. On the adventure shows, the hero protects the diagnosed sick, and the watching child learns another diagnosis. On the comedy program, the joke sometimes deals with an illness or a handicap, real or imaginary, sad or comical, and each time the watching and listening child learns more about the meaning of diagnostic labels. As television spreads across the world, this medium has undoubtedly become the main avenue whereby children learn the meaning of diagnoses.

In his day-to-day social experience, the growing child is also learning the significance of diagnostic terms. His brothers, sisters, cousins and friends have illnesses that are given names; these children get better or they die, so the child learns what these disease labels mean. Parents, grandparents, neighbors and friends are stricken by sicknesses that are diagnosed and discussed, and the listening, watching child is taught. Relatives whisper the word "cancer" and weep. Youngsters learn by watching their reactions and by sensing their feelings. Grandfather has a "heart attack," uncle has a "stroke," aunt has a "lump in the breast," and slowly but surely over the years, the growing child learns the meaning of illness and illness outcomes and comes to attach increasing significance to diagnostic terms.

Children learn the meaning of diagnosis in different ways in different cultures. For the young white American, the term "sickle-cell disease" may have meaning only in early adolescence, when he moves outside his ethnic group. To the black American, this diagnosis has major personal impact from an early childhood age. Fortunately, meningitis, tuberculosis, cholera and malaria are diagnoses that will have little social significance in the industrialized nations, but they are fraught with personal meaning to children in the developing nations. A British grade school child can listen now to a family discussion of tuberculosis without feeling menaced. At the turn of the century, tuberculosis was a widespread and dreaded disease in Britain, and very young children learned then what dread significance this term had. In the underdeveloped nations, tuberculosis is still one of the captains of death, and children there are taught early to fear this diagnosis.

Most children begin to understand the diagnoses of the common fatal illnesses in their culture from the time they are about five years old, and during the grade school years, youngsters become increasingly aware of the impact of fatal illnesses. As they grow older, they learn what diagnoses mean and are more likely to understand the significance of these terms when they themselves are diagnosed.

The Prognosis

To understand the personal meaning of his prognosis, to appreciate what an illness will do to him, the growing child must be able to think in more abstract ways. He has to appreciate the meaning of time present and time future. To comprehend the meaning of the prognosis, he has to be able to imagine and to visualize in his mind possible physical change and deterioration. He has to have the intellectual ability to understand that he carries this illness process within himself and that this sickness will eventually produce changes in his body and his existence.

For a four- or five-year-old child, the disease prognosis is still a concept beyond his level of understanding. The six-year-old youngster and, much more, the seven-year-old is starting to think over a time sequence and is more able to imagine. By seven years of age, the growing child is becoming able to conceptualize what might be and what can become, and so a disease prognosis becomes something of meaning to the school-aged child.

If a four-year-old child learns that his disease prognosis is for a three months' survival (that is he is likely to die in three months time), he may appear to be outwardly unconcerned. At four years of age, a child does not have the intellectual ability to understand the meaning of three months as a span of time. He has no intellectual grasp of the significance of future time. Three months to a child of this age could be years and years away, in a time of perhaps and maybe. On the other hand, this four-year-old child may become very upset when he learns his disease has a three months' survival prognosis, because he feels he is going to die now, tonight or tomorrow. Three months to such a youngster may mean this evening or tomorrow morning. He is liable to fear that this dreadful thing called death may envelop him before breakfast or even tonight when he is going to sleep. To make sure that he does not die, he may decide not to take his clothes off and to stay awake. He is liable to become panicky and distraught. The four-year-old lives now, in the present. Only as he grows older and develops understanding of the continuity of time will he be able to project events forward into the future and to anticipate and fantasize.

By seven years of age, when a youngster normally has a beginning age-appropriate understanding of time sequence, the child has more ability to appreciate what his illness process will mean in terms of time duration. Other factors, however, will influence his response to the prognosis. At this grade school age, the child is still dependent on his parents for final guidance, and to such a youngster, a diagnosis and a prognosis by a physician is a prediction, almost a command, by a powerful parentlike person. When a parental person such as a doctor or nurse tells him that he will die in three months, the seven-year-old child is liable to feel that this statement is an absolute cut and dried decision. The seven-year-old then may respond to learning the prognosis as if he had been sentenced to an inescapable fate. If an elementary school child is told in some way that his illness is liable to have a three months' duration, he may wait for fate to strike him down exactly three months later. He is likely to respond as if he has been given a date of execution and watch the calendar and mark off each day in his mind. The young school child can become so anxious about the meaning of his prognosis that he is drained emotionally and physically and becomes less able to deal with the stress of his illness.

In dealing with the dying child, parents, family and caring personnel must appreciate that, by the early grade school years, many children can understand the full significance of the prognosis. Emotional and intellectual maturity and increasing knowledge in this way add to the emotional burdens of the dying child. As the youngster grows older, he has greater emotional and intellectual capability, but he is also faced more directly with the meaning of his illness. Even though the child is older and more mature, he may need more support to help him cope with the added emotional task that comes with understanding what the prognosis of his illness really means.

Many children and adults, of course, never do develop a mature time sense and always live in the present. They live now, and they never worry about the future until the future has become their present. Children and adolescents who develop emotionally in this present-focused way may still be relatively unconcerned on learning the prognosis of their illness. Their way of coping is not to worry about anything that does not happen today. They may be able, more comfortably, to accept emotionally the illness prognosis even though intellectually they are capable of knowing the total impact of their disease.

Change in Social Role and Relationships

When the child begins to understand what death will mean to him, he can also appreciate that dying will change the relationships he has developed. While the youngster is developing increasing awareness of his separate identity and his unique place in his family and culture, he is becoming more able to understand that death will mean for him a separation from these familiar and loved persons and the loss of these meaningful relationships he has enjoyed. As the child grows older, his increasing intellectual sophistication allows him to realize that death will separate him from those he loves.

A three-year-old can still be relatively unconcerned when he hears the people around him talking about his impending death. He can hear the words. He can watch and participate in his diagnosis and treatment. He may not really like what is happening to him, but in the long run, he feels safe in the protection and guidance of his parents. He knows that he is cared for, loved and guarded. With little anxiety, he can play with his toys and his pets while other family members discuss the fact that the child is dying.

With an older child, this situation is different. A seven-year-old youngster is likely to be deeply distressed at the idea that he is dying because he can look at his family and know now that he will be separated from them in death. He may not be sure yet where he will go when he is dead or for how long he will be dead, but at age seven, he does know that separation is inevitable in death. He does not want to leave his family. At seven years of age, he does not want his parents and family to leave him. He is likely to be angry if he is told that he will be happier "up there" in heaven. He is already happy down here on earth and does not want to leave this happiness. He is apt to be resentful if he is told that God is taking him home to be with Him. The seven-year-old is liable to retort that he does not want God; he is quite happy at home with his parents and family, and he does not want to leave them. He does not really accept the idea that death is a form of sleep because he is enjoying being very much awake. From about five years of age and most certainly by seven years, the child who is dying knows that he is about to lose the warm and loving relationships he has. He may be told that this loss is only temporary, but he appreciates that he cannot avoid a separation. The grade school child has to mourn, with understandable sadness and anger, the fact that his relationships are bound to change when he dies. As part of normal growth and development, the seven-year-old child has developed a secure self-concept of himself as an individual and as a member of his family and community, so he has also developed the ability to appreciate that his death will mean that he will be separated from these very important relationships.

Every dying person, even a child, has to face the fact that in each culture there is a socially acceptable way to die. This accepted pattern of dying varies between cultures and across social groups. As the child lives through the process of dying and death, he will learn from the reactions of the people around him how he is expected to die. He will find that certain of his responses to his illness and death are acceptable (this varies with his culture), while other feelings must be hidden, lest people become anxious, angry or upset. If he is Scottish, Scandinavian or a staunch New Englander, he will quickly come to understand that his stoic acceptance of dying is expected. If he is Irish, Jewish or Italian, he is certainly allowed and indeed expected to seek caring and comfort. In the hospital and in his home, he will be taught how to die as a "good patient" or a "good son." In most hospitals, he will learn quickly not to talk too openly about his death because treating personnel, fellow patients and his family members are likely to become very anxious and upset with this kind of conversation. Patients who are too honest about their weakness or pain find that they are considered to be "bad patients." The child who is dying will soon appreciate that he cannot show open wounds or talk too directly about the pain he suffers because the people around him, who cannot soothe or comfort him as they would like, become much too tense when he reminds them of their powerlessness. Even at home, a dying child will learn that his family members will be much more comfortable and happy if he dies cooperatively. The dying youngster will find his parents, his relatives and the people who treat him respond much more readily to his few fleeting smiles than to his angry outbursts. Frequently, the fatally ill youngster comes to realize that he cannot act like a child when he is dying. As he moves towards death, the youngster will learn that increasingly he gives up or loses control of his life. He does what others want, and he waits till they are ready. If he is dying a "good death," he does not complain, and he accepts. Many youngsters become quieter and more withdrawn as their final days near.

In death, the young child finds that he has an unavoidable role to play in his family and his culture. From the age of five or six and frequently even younger, most children live out this social role as they move through the process from life to death.

The Task of Dying

As the child grows older, he learns more about himself and his place in his universe. He comes to appreciate the mystery, the burden and the challenge of death. Once the child has achieved this understanding, this knowledge stays with him as long as he lives—the death agony, the reality of disease, diagnosis and prognosis, the meaning of separation and death and the dying role in his culture. As he matures, the youngster comes to learn the deeper meanings of both life and death, and his living is enriched by his knowledge. His dying also can be more meaningful because he now understands more. Everyone who deals with the dying child must be aware of what level of understanding and emotional growth he has reached so that, as he dies, they can help him achieve the maximum comfort, the greatest security and the deepest closeness.

Chapter Two

THE PRESCHOOL CHILD

In the industrialized nations, death in very young children is most often caused by congenital malformations, by injury around the time of birth, by infections, by accidents at home and at play, by malignancies and by leukemia. The prime causes of early childhood death in the developing countries are still the infections and perinatal trauma.

The newborn infant may be so handicapped by physical deformity or birth injury that he quickly succumbs—a fleeting visitor to this life. The child who is born with the physical burden of a severe congenital defect may find that he cannot cope physiologically with the increasing demands that come with growth; eventually he dies, overwhelmed by the added stress of growth. Especially in the less advanced nations, the young child is susceptible to gastrointestinal inflammations, to the meningitides and to pneumonic infections; his uncertain existence is easily overwhelmed by the intrusion of environmental infection.

As the youngster grows and ventures forth on his own, he faces new opportunity for adventure, for intellectual growth and for death. The open door and the beckoning window, the kitchen closet with the fascinating bottles and their lethal contents, the roadway in which the cars speed by, exciting, inviting and fatal. With each new step towards maturity, the child inevitably is faced with greater threats to his life. The quick childish hand that eagerly seizes the candy can also reach out unexpectedly for the boiling kettle. The infant who is able to crawl around the room and under the table is also capable of creeping across to the crackling fire or under the family car. At the same time that the toddler proudly learns to use the toilet by himself, he also achieves a more private access to the bathroom medicine cabinet.

The skills that the kindergarten child learns on the school pegboard can be readily applied to the knobs and the buttons on the kitchen stove. The natural processes of growth bring every child a wider opportunity for life and for death.

The newborn infant reacts to the physical stress of dying with all his innate physiological reflexes. Instinctively his whole body strives to maintain life as long as possible in face of the death agony. At this very young age, the infant tries with every fiber of his existence to relieve these intolerable inner tensions. He is barely aware of the world outside himself and, at this time in life, only dimly knows how to seek caring. He relates to people and to things around him through touch, smell and sound. He does not think in terms of words but responds rather to voice tones. If he feels pain, hunger or breathlessness, he cries out in immediate anxiety. If his tension is not quickly relieved, his cry becomes more distressed, then panicky and finally may subside into a beaten whimper. The warmth of his mother's bosom may settle him for a time, but this comfort may not be enough to relieve his continuing inner physical tensions. The pleasure of the nipple, the warmth of the milk and the gentleness of his mother's arms will soothe him temporarily, but then the pain and the unease return once more and persist. Medications can give some relief, but frequently, drugs do not totally take away his inner misery unless the little child is sedated to the point of anesthesia. His parents, his babushka, his nurse and his physician can make his journey through death easier by providing some physical relief and comfort (Duff, 1976); as they watch their young child die, the family of the fatally ill infant need a great deal of support while they struggle with their feelings of helplessness (Kennell, 1970). In the same way, treatment team members may feel guilty or depressed when they realize that they are of so little purpose to the dying infant. The child who dies in the first weeks of life travels much of this journey alone.

When the infant has grown to be several months of age, he has started to develop an ability to interact more directly with the people around him. He smiles and coos, and he learns that he can produce warmth and attention from his family. He cuddles into mother's body; he reacts comfortably to the sense of her physical nearness, and soon he begins to respond directly and specifically to her as a person. Gradually from two or three months of age and much more obviously by five or six months, the growing child shows fear at the presence of people who are not his mother. By his anxious responses, he is indicating that he can appreciate, albeit dimly, that these people are different from mother. The child's father may become concerned and sometimes even guilty when he realizes that his five-month-old child is scared of him. In the next few months of life, however, the youngster gradually becomes comfortable and secure with father also and then with other family members. The growing infant has started to differentiate amongst people and now react to them in different ways.

The preschool child handles his own dying with the primitive understanding and the very limited emotional responses of the very young. The infant and the toddler are dependent on parents and those around for their very existence—for food, for guidance and for basic day-to-day decisions. The young child relies on his parents for direction as to what he should do and even how he should feel. Only gradually, by experience and by example during the preschool years, the child learns whether he should touch, how he should go and whether it is safe. In a slow and sometimes painful process, the growing child is taught acceptable and appropriate patterns of reacting—when something is funny, when something is sad. The young preschool child does not yet understand death nor has he learned how to react to dying. The toddler can play happily with the flowers that are arranged on top of the coffin because he does not understand the significance of this box. He may admire the smoothness and shininess of the wood. He is liable to amuse himself by breathing on this unusual piece of furniture and drawing faces in the mist. He does not realize that he is expected to react in any other way and will become confused and upset if family members respond with anger at his behavior. He is just doing what a child naturally does at his age level.

The preschool child is likely to feel sad and upset because his family is sad and upset, but he himself is not really mourning because he does not know the significance of death. The three-year-old will respond with anger and sadness when important people are not there, but he does not worry just because someone is dying. His world is his mother, his father and his immediate family. He reflects the feelings of the people who are important in his life. He is only learning to have feelings of his own.

As he grows, the young child needs first to be told and shown, then he experiments repeatedly on his own with support and encouragement, and finally, he develops sufficient personality strength to make his own decisions and to express his own feelings. This process of evolving independence and developing self-sufficiency is only beginning in the preschool years. When the young child of this age is faced with his own fatal illness, he is almost totally dependent on the people who care for him and love him for whatever understanding he has of what is happening. He watches his parents, his family and the people who treat him and takes his cues from them as to how he should respond to this new situation. His personal dying has meaning to the preschool child primarily as it affects the people around him.

When the toddler is hospitalized, he is faced with the fact that he has been separated from the people and places he knows and on whom he depends. He realizes that he is small and that he needs his mother, his father and his family, and he responds acutely to this separation. When the family are not there, the young child seeks desperately the familiar face that guarantees security. With his searching eyes, his awkward hands and his whole groping body, he struggles to find again someone who is familiar, someone who is secure, someone who will guide him. Strange faces do not bring comfort but rather cause him increasing anxiety. The child knows that these people are different. They sound different. They smell different. They even feel different. He does not understand them. He does not trust them. He does not know what to do. His tension mounts. His frantic searching increases. His cries become more strident. His restlessness is liable to grow more frantic, until finally it exhausts him. He knows only that the familiar, loving people who take care of him are not there. He is separated from his mother, his father and family and without them the toddler is unable to cope.

To add to the emotional burdens of separation, the young child in the hospital is faced with a totally strange environment. He has to eat when they give him food, not when he wants. He has to eat their food, and it tastes strange. He has to sleep in their bed, which does not mold to his body as his bed does. To add to the nightmare, these people in the hospital, these strange adults, cause him pain (Morrissey, 1963). They stick needles into his body. They probe him with tubes. They handle him roughly. They do not have time to play with him when he wants or change him when he is soiled. They do not understand what he is trying to tell them. Their voices and words are different, and their language is more distant. When they do lift him up, he realizes that their strange bodies do not have the feel or the responsiveness that is mother.

Soon he learns to associate these strangers with repeated unpleasant experiences. He quickly recognizes that pain tends to occur when these unknown hands, these faces in uniforms, approach. Even at age four, five or six months, the young child readily becomes conditioned to react with fear to people in white coats. After a white coat has stuck a needle in his veins or his muscles several times, the child has been taught very specifically that white coats are unpleasant. He will scream when the nurse lowers the side of his bed because he knows that the squeal of the descending bedside precedes the pain of an injection. He has heard this noise before; he has felt the pain several times; he has learned. The toddler shrinks away in fear from the smiling doctor's face because he has come to recognize that these looming eyes precede the pain-provoking hands that change the dressing. These fear reactions to white coats and to treating personnel may persist throughout a child's illness and make a prolonged and difficult treatment program even more complicated. Sensitive clinical staff may become very upset when they realize that their patients fear them.

When a child under three years of age is hospitalized, the treatment staff must appreciate that this youngster needs his parents and family with him so that he can cope reasonably with unfamiliar people, painful experiences and unpredictable situations. He needs his mother so that he can feel safe. He needs his father to protect him. He needs his family to tell him what he should do. If he has his mother, or his parenting person, the child will be much more able to cooperate in his treatment. For a two- or three-year-old youngster, father, grandparents or even brothers and sisters may take mother's place in helping the young child to cope with the stresses of hospitalization. These familiar people can be with him so that he does not feel absolutely alone and helpless. They can stay with him and help him endure. They can comfort him and help make the pain bearable; they can "kiss and make it better."

Mother and other close family members can encourage and cajole the child so that he takes the food that he needs for his strength. They can help the nursing staff carry out the medical orders, and sometimes family members can do the nursing chores. They can soothe the youngster so that his anxiety is relieved, and he sleeps more peacefully. Mother, father and family members may want to introduce members of the treatment team to the child so that the child accepts them almost as members of the family. In this way, the youngster can feel more comfortable and secure with the clinical personnel and more able to use them as parent or family substitutes. With the cooperation and the help of the family, treating personnel may gradually become accepted by the young child and more able to comfort, to help and to treat him. In some of the developing nations where nursing professionals are unavailable, mother and family members actually move into the hospital with the child. Under these circumstances, young children show far fewer fear responses and are much better able to cooperate in difficult and even painful diagnostic and treatment procedures. When mother sleeps in the same hospital bed as the child, the toddler can feel safe.

The toddler and the preschool child cannot understand what death will mean to them. As far as the young child appreciates, he and his mother and his father are a family unit that will continue forever. He does not have to worry that his life and his existence may come to an end because, as far as he understands life, he lives in the timeless security of his parents, and they in him. Not only does the young child react to the physical discomfort and the pain that may come as part of the illness and his treatment, but he also responds to the sadness and the worries of his father and mother. His parents' feelings are quickly communicated to the child and become his feelings. When the mother realizes that the child is dying and is sad, the child will be sad. Since the mother clings more intensely to her youngster because she knows he will leave her in death, the child will cling more desperately to his mother because he senses from her that somehow a separation is coming. When the grieving father looks at his young daughter and his eyes fill with tears, the little girl who is dying will be sad, although she will not know exactly why her spirits are low. Because the feelings of the parents and the family are communicated so readily to the child and in this way become the child's emotions, the task of dying often becomes much more difficult for the youngster. Young children will respond with fear as they get nearer death, not because they can understand the fearfulness of death, but rather because their parents are fearful.

While the young child finds it frightening when he is hospitalized and separated from his family, his parents may also find that their separation from the child is very difficult to accept. When he leaves them, they worry that they may never see him again in his home. Parents often feel that hospitalization is the first of the final steps in the total separation that comes with death. The separation anxiety and the fears of the parents increase the tension that the dying child feels and may make the youngster's hospitalization even more difficult for everyone to endure. If the parents can participate actively in the child's hospital treatment program in some meaningful way (Hamovitch, 1964), they frequently feel less anxious and more useful. When the child's father and mother are more at peace, the youngster then can relax more easily and handle a difficult situation with greater competence. If treating personnel spend time to help the child's family cope with their fears and anxieties about his approaching death, the child himself will become much more settled and need less nursing attention.

When the devout Muslim parent can say with certainty, "It is God's will," and accept the fact that his child is dying, the preschool Arabic child can accept more easily. Where the Christian parent believes that his dying child will pass beyond and be "safe in the arms of Jesus," the parent then can feel much more secure, and the child feels safe. In the nonreligious populations in the socialist countries, death is liable to be viewed as a final, permanent separation. Parents in these countries believe that the child's death means an absolute farewell, and under these circumstances, their separation anxiety and mourning is accentuated. To protect parents and families from this separation stress, Soviet clinicians tend to withhold a fatal diagnosis as long as possible. They know the separation between the dying youngster and his parents and relatives is likely to be distressing for the staff, the family and the child.

As the youngster grows older, he becomes increasingly capable and able to act on his own. He begins to decide for himself and to express his own opinions. More and more the growing child enjoys this new feeling of power and revels in this experience of mastery. He finds he can do things and succeed. He realizes he can state his wishes and get what he wants. He starts to say No at times just for the pleasant feeling of being different, opposite and individualistic. He begins to resist the demands of other people. Sometimes he defies his parents and his family just for the pleasure of self-assertion. He rejects the advice of those around him so that he can have the satisfaction of making his own decisions and of expressing himself, sometimes even against the wishes of the parents he loves. He refuses assistance so that he can now "do it myself," even though he may be turning down something he really does want. The maturing preschool child enjoys being forceful and aggressive. He likes to use his own energy doing what he wants. A child at this age may even behave so aggressively in his play he injures his pets or even his playmates. Injury is merely an incidental result of his new self-assertiveness (Anthony, 1940). The preschool child is discovering with wonderment and gratification the pleasures of independence and mastery, of building and destroying.

At this developmental stage of life when the child is only two or three years of age, he sees everything in the world as neatly black or white. Everything is divided into those things which are all good and those things which are all bad. People and children are nice, or they are not nice. Daddy is felt to be completely bad "and I wish he was dead," that is, somewhere away from me, next door or down the block, but somewhere where he can come back when he is good and forgiven. Alternatively, Daddy is totally wonderful, and "I want him all to myself," completely and absolutely, at this moment, now. Mommy is seen as the most beautiful woman in the world who smells so nice, or Mommy is a nasty, mean old witch. Everything is clearly defined, and there are no shades of gray in the way the three-year-old child sees his world. At this developmental period, the youngster tends to react totally in one direction or totally in the other, and he anticipates that the rest of the world deals with him in this same all or nothing fashion.

As this young child is developing his own independence and his new self-assertiveness, he has thoughts that he knows are angry or even bad. In his young mind, bad thoughts can cause bad things to happen in a magical fashion. He does not yet have the intellectual and emotional ability to understand that he can have thoughts without these thoughts being a solid reality. He does not recognize that he can have bad wishes and keep these feelings all to himself without something bad happening. The young child cannot appreciate that his ideas are not being read by those all-powerful parents and adults. He knows he can read his own thoughts, so he believes that, in some fashion, his parents can read his mind also. If he has these naughty and angry ideas and feelings, he thinks that Mommy and Daddy can see what is going through his mind and may very well decide to punish him because he deserves to be punished for bad thoughts. Since any normal child of this age, who is beginning to be independent, does have at times angry, negativistic and rebellious thoughts, he is liable to believe that there are many reasons why he deserves to be punished, even a punishment such as being sent away to a hospital or being subjected to the pain of medical and surgical treatments.

The very young child has no understanding of chance. He cannot appreciate that some things occur naturally and spontaneously. In his mind, he lives in a world where everything happens because someone is doing something to someone else. Thus, when the toddler is hospitalized for an illness that will eventually be fatal, he is likely to feel that this separation from his home and his family is a punishment, and of course, he knows very well that he has had bad thoughts, and he may believe that his bad thoughts brought on this deserved punishment. He realizes that he has been taken away from his home—a punishment. He feels that a punishment only comes when badness has been present. Thus, he must have been very bad to bring on this kind of treatment. He feels that this separation, this hospitalization, is one way his parents and his family are punishing him. He is liable to blame himself for deserving this punishment. Mommy and Daddy have sent him away because he has been bad, angry and disobedient.

In response to his hospitalization, the young child is prone to blame himself for being sent away from home and is apt to react in childish guilt, sadness and withdrawal. The necessary but painful physical treatment procedures in the hospital merely confirm to him that he is still being punished for those nasty words and disobedient thoughts. He is likely then to feel even more guilty and deserving of punishment because he is now being angry at his parents for rejecting him and for allowing him to suffer these painful experiences which somehow he feels he should deserve. The preschool child in hospital or undergoing outpatient treatment will need a great deal of parental reassurance that he has not been bad and that he is not being punished. By their actions and words, his parents must emphasize to him that they are not angry with him and that they do love him very much. They understand that he does not like his hospitalization, and they appreciate that he is angry at being away from his family and his home. They can help the preschool child understand that they, too, in their own way, do not like the fact that he is ill and feel deprived because he has been taken from them. They know how much he misses them because they miss him very much.

Parents should stay with the child who is hospitalized or receiving treatment as much as they can, and they should bring with them his familiar toys, pictures and books to minimize the feelings of strangeness and separation. No matter how much the parents may reassure the toddler, he will continue to have doubts. The youngster at this age does not have the intellectual ability to make sense of all the medical procedures, no matter how much his parents and the treatment staff try to explain. Even adults, even health professionals, cannot understand all the hospital apparatus and techniques when they are hospitalized. The young child finds it difficult, at times impossible, to believe that these towering x-ray machines are not dangerous and threatening and these people with the masks are not hiding their faces for some sinister purpose—just like the outlaw he saw in the movies.

Since he blames himself for this separation and feels that the hospitalization and the treatment are a punishment that he somehow deserves, the child tends to keep his anger within himself or to direct it, not at his parents with whom he is angry, but at the treating staff or at other young patients on the hospital unit. The more the youngster misses his home, the more likely he is to be nasty towards the child in the next bed. The more the young child cares for his parents, the more he suffers from being separated from them and the more angry he is liable to be at the hospital staff. His irritability will then make the treatment personnel angry at him, so as a result, the youngster feels even worse about himself. His wickedness has now been confirmed. The child aged two or three, burdened with his loneliness, anger and guilt, finds it very difficult to handle these feelings by himself when he is hospitalized. At this young age, he is still very dependent on his parents to help him know what to do and how to handle his feelings. Since he still needs his mother and his father to help him understand, he now finds himself angry and resentful towards the very people he needs and cannot do without. These young children require all the help and support they can get. Parents, grandparents, brothers, sisters, aunts and uncles must be encouraged individually or in turn to be with the young hospitalized child as much as is reasonably possible, depending on the child's physical strength and on the requirements of the hospital treatment procedures.

However, a child of this tender age cannot cope with more than one or two family members at a time, so the whole clan should not descend on him all at once. With too many people around his bed, the toddler will become confused, tired and irritable. The attention of one or two trusted family members helps the young child recognize that he is not being rejected by his family, even though he suspects that he is. If his parents visit him frequently in the hospital, he comes to realize that his angry thoughts are not driving them away; somehow his thoughts do not have that force. He learns that his father and mother still love him. If the young child continues secure in the love of his parents and family and confident that he is not being abandoned, he may then be more able to express his understandable anger at his being hospitalized away from home. He has good reason to be furious at what is happening to him, but it is only with the support and the comfort of his parents and family that he can feel safe enough to allow himself to be angry.

Loving parents are sometimes shocked and deeply hurt when they find that their young child responds to their frequent visits with repeated angry outbursts or even by bitter physical abuse. While parents should not tolerate aggressive behavior or unending anger, they must appreciate that only a relatively secure, self-confident child could allow himself to express the anger he feels or show the resentment caused by his separation and hospitalization. If the preschool child was uncertain of his parents' love or felt totally alone in the world, he would be less able to express these feelings; it would not be safe. In many instances, the anger of the hospitalized preschool child is an outward sign of emotional security (Adams, 1976).

If the preschool child is showing his separation anger, the parents, the family and the treatment staff should try to help him channel his resentment in a productive fashion. While the mother and father recognize that their child's ability to show understandable bitterness is a sign of emotional strength, they certainly do not need to let him express this anger towards them in an unrealistic fashion. No parent should allow any child, however sick, to hit or kick him. Parents should not permit themselves to be assaulted or misused by a child, physically or verbally. While parents let the youngster know that they understand the reasons for his anger, at the same time they must continue to teach him that it is not all right to be continually nasty. When the young child has the emotional strength and security to show his anger, he can be helped to channel this normal reaction productively in pounding a pegboard, in splashing paint on paper, in crashing toy cars together. If he is emotionally secure enough to show his annoyance at his hospitalization, he can fight this separation from his family by working hard to do more things for himself. His family members can encourage him to use his aggressiveness in working to stay well or to beat his symptoms.

Parental participation in day-to-day hospital procedures minimizes the anxieties and guilt that both the child and his parents have when they are separated and not able to be of use to each other (Knudson and Natterson, 1960; Hamovitch, 1964). Parents can certainly help to feed and dress their child. They can take the youngster for walks within the hospital, on the hospital grounds or even on short trips away from the hospital. They can play with the child and so free staff time for other professional duties. Family members can carry out simple medical and nursing procedures under supervision and direction of the staff. In this way the child comes to appreciate that his parents and he are members of the treatment team along with the doctors and the nurses. Everyone is working together for his good.

While it helps the preschool child feel much more secure when parents and relatives stay with him around the clock, the parents do need time away from the child so that they can continue to be parents to other family members. The parents should be expected to leave the child periodically so that they can continue their own lives away from the dying child. The treating staff must be very careful to see that the parents do not sacrifice themselves and the rest of the family for this one child who is dying. Even though parents are encouraged to visit as much as possible, they should leave during the afternoon nap or in the evenings when the child is asleep. The members of the family can stay with the child in turn rather than all together. In their absence, they can leave behind familiar, easily recognizable tokens and mementoes of the home and the family—favorite toys and pictures, that old tattered blanket, that well-fingered book, a plate of cookies.

As the preschool child grows older, he begins to develop an awareness of himself as an individual and a separate human being. He starts to realize that, somehow, he is someone all on his own. He learns by testing out his own strengths and perceptions that he has a physical body that belongs to him alone. He finds out, by expressing his opinions and sharing his feelings, that he has a personality that is distinct and different from other people and from other things around him. During this time that the growing child is developing this awareness of his separate identify, he is also starting to appreciate dimly that, if he does indeed exist as something separate and individual, he can cease to exist. When he begins to understand this very important reality that he has a separate and unique identity, at the same time he must start to face the inescapable fact that this individuality may, in some fashion at some time, come to an end. At the same time he learns that he lives as an individual, the growing child starts to comprehend that he can die as an individual.

During this period from two to four years of age, the growing youngster comes to understand the meaning of "myself" and "I." While he is appreciating more and more that he is indeed a "me," he is starting to realize that "me" can become "not me." This new understanding of existence brings with it the deepest and most profound form of human anxiety—the awareness that an individual can cease to exist. Most human beings find it difficult to think for any extended time about the fact that sometime they will no longer continue in this physical world. Such thoughts give rise to very disturbing anxiety. It is difficult for any man or woman, adult or child, to tolerate the thought that his or her personal existence may cease. Very dimly, from the second year of life, and gradually, but to an increasing extent over the next two or three years, the growing child develops an understanding and appreciation of possible nonexistence. Such a thought is very tension provoking to the young child, just as it is to any other human being, and has to be shut out—denied—so that the child can continue to think of other more tolerable and more productive topics.

This new understanding of personal separateness and vulnerability is normally kept out of awareness because such thoughts would make the youngster much too anxious. Thus, the child who at three years of age could talk blithely about dying may appear totally disinterested in the same subject when he becomes four or five years old. He now blots out these ideas and feelings and avoids the topic of death. While a very young child can crush an ant or destroy a flower without any worry, this same child a few years later may become very protective of living creatures and growing objects because he now understands the fuller significance of life and not-life—the significance that now involves him in a very personal fashion.

Even though the four- or five-year-old youngster may appear outwardly unconcerned about death or dying because he has trained himself not to think about such topics, the stress placed on him by this new awareness will nevertheless show. When his own physical existence is threatened by a fatal illness, outwardly the five-year-old may seem unconcerned. Though he may not allow himself to think about death, his nightmares—those horrible feelings of being overwhelmed—may increase. While he may show no apparent concern about his illness or the course of his treatment, his games may become more violent and destructive. In her doll play, the little girl may show much more interest in accidents and disasters or even with hospitals and funerals. The little boy's games with his toy soldiers often become more bloodthirsty and destructive. However, the youngster's emotional denial is likely to be maintained even in the play. The soldiers, the Indians and the painted figures come back to life and continue living. They die, but they do not cease to exist. In this play, the young child reassures himself that his newly achieved independence and individuality does not come to an end; it cannot, it must not. But always there is that nagging question, "Will it?" By manipulating and arranging his toys and by deciding the fate of his playthings, the young child shows himself that he still can control his own existence. The youngster should be allowed to continue this play because these outlets for his fears and anxieties permit him a healthy tension release. His natural denial must be supported and tolerated. The young preschool child, like most human beings, needs to cover over and suppress feelings and ideas that otherwise are impossible to handle.

If the preschool child is comfortable enough to ask about his illness, he should be told only what he asks. He should not be burdened with more details than his childish mind can grasp. He must not be given ideas and facts that he cannot understand, and he will indicate by his questions what he can handle. The questions the preschool child asks are a form of reaching out for support and understanding. Thus, if the five-year-old asks at the beginning of his illness, "Am I going to die?" the answer could be, "No, you are not going to die right now." This response supports the child's need to deny but equally tells him truthfully what will happen today or tomorrow. The preschool child must always be dealt with on this basis of day-to-day reality. He is unable to understand something that may happen three months from now or even two weeks hence. He needs to be told about today and tomorrow and possibly about the day after in simple, truthful facts.

If the youngster asks, "Will it hurt?" he should be answered honestly. If the procedure indeed will be painful, he can be told,

"Yes, it will hurt, but we will try to do it as quickly as possible. If you keep very still, it will not hurt quite as much." When the child wonders whether an operation is likely to be painful, he should be given a truthful answer. He can be told directly that his stomach will hurt for a while after the operation, but he will be given medicine to help make the pain better. Often the child feels much safer when he knows how his treatment program is planned. If he understands that he gets his pills when the small hand of the clock is at five, this knowledge gives him some more security and certainty. Even though he does not like to have his dressings changed, this treatment procedure is easier to tolerate when he understands that it happens only on every second day. He can mark his free days on that calendar at the end of the bed. It helps the young child in the hospital to cope if he knows when his mother will be coming to see him, how many hours she will stay and when she will leave. He should know that Mommy will arrive at nine o'clock in the morning, after his breakfast and his medicine, and will stay all afternoon and evening until he is ready to go to sleep. The young patient should know that Daddy will be there at five o'clock, just after he finishes work, and will stay until the night nurse comes on duty, and so on. These young patients in the hospital need predictability and stability because they are living in a situation where they wear strange clothes, eat unfamiliar food and live by impersonal hospital routines. Frequently, they have nothing to do to fill the hospital hours except worry.

As the process of dying moves irretrievably onward, the preschool child may be less able to blot out his awareness that somehow his existence is threatened. He can feel changes happening within him and to him. Even though his questions are answered truthfully by his family and the caring staff, the responses are not quite as confident, as definite or as happy as he would like. The people who love him are unable to give him the absolute security he wishes because, as he senses, in the long run there are no absolute answers to questions about his situation.

When the approach of death becomes more obvious and the child asks again, "Am I going to die?" the answer should be, as always, truthful and direct. When death may indeed come today, tomorrow or the day after, the child and his family finally have to face this truth. His parents and the treating staff continue to be the greatest support to him if they still respond on the basis of the child's reality. When death is actually happening to the child, it should be acknowledged at that time. The parents and the caring staff can reply to his questions, "Yes, you are going to die, but we will look after you." The preschool child has lived in the security of his parents' protection and should die with the same support. If he is certain that his parents will still care for him, no matter what happens, the dying child will be better able to go to his final rest still happy and comforted.

Even with the support and the love of his parents and family, the four- or five-year-old will be unable to deny absolutely the process that is occurring to him as he approaches death. He may find it much more difficult to control all his tensions and anxieties. He will sense that his parents are becoming more anxious and sad. He will note that, as death comes nigh, those around him are withdrawing. As his final hours grow nearer, the child's emotional and physical strength becomes less. His behavior may become less mature and more infantile. This emotional regression sometimes makes the process of dying more bearable for the child. If the youngster does give up some of the emotional and intellectual maturity he has developed and becomes more like a toddler or infant, he is allowing himself to go back to that earlier growth stage where he is more dependent on his parents. Death then loses its threat to his personal existence. When the dying child regresses emotionally to the stage where he again depends on his parents for total decision making, he no longer has to worry that he will in some way cease to exist physically. At this more childlike level of development, he can now live in the security and the comfort of his parents. He will be less anxious because he feels once more that he and his parents live as one unit and live forever. Parents, family and treating staff should allow and support the child's regression to a younger age level of functioning because, at this more infantile stage, the dying youngster can feel safer and more secure during this final period of his life.

However, some preschool children are unwilling or unable to allow themselves to become childlike again. They keep themselves fiercely independent, even if this independence means that they have to face the anxieties of death. If the four- or five-year-old child is mature for his age and enjoys the new pleasures of independence, he is apt to be reluctant to give this up. Because he has become accustomed to doing things for himself and to making his own decisions, he may not be able to allow himself to be babied. Some youngsters cannot permit themselves to be treated like very young children again because their childhood was not very happy. If the dying child has had difficult or painful experiences with his parents and family when he was younger, he may be fearful of becoming a dependent child once more. Alone, independent and facing death, such a child may show outward signs of his mounting anxiety in his increasingly loud and aggressive behavior. Since he now knows that something unpleasant is happening to him, something that his childish mind cannot totally comprehend, he may believe that things are being done against him. The overly independent preschool child may express his anxieties by blaming the people around him and may actually become suspicious and untrusting of the treatment personnel and even his own family. In face of his anxieties, his anger and his suspiciousness, the preschool child who insists on maintaining his independence may be forced to cope with his awareness of approaching death in the only way left to him, by withdrawing into his own private world, populated by his own imagination—a world of wish-fulfillment, private fantasy and inevitable happy endings. The five-year-old child who does not, or cannot, handle his final anxieties by becoming more childlike, regressed and dependent is more likely to end his days withdrawn in his own daydream world.

As the preschool child grows, he learns the meaning of death from what he sees in his day-to-day experience. He is taught about death by the squirrel lying squashed at the roadside. He learns about death when he brings a baby bird home and finds that it does not survive his loving care. He is instructed about death on the television screen when he sees his nation's leaders lying in state and carried to their final resting place. In the movies and on his favorite television shows, he watches his heroes writhe in their dying anguish. Even though his parents often refuse to give him direct data about the meaning and the reality of death (Wahl, 1958), he still learns this information from his family.

In American society, grandparents are put on display, old and motionless in their caskets, waiting for that final family kiss of duty before they disappear forever. The child looks at his grandfather lying there and watches his family, and he learns. Aunts and uncles go off to the hospital and never come back; they have died, and people cry, and the growing child remembers. Sometimes death provides an even more personal lesson. A father may be alive and happy one day but fatally injured in a work accident the next. A mother may waste away physically with a progressive malignancy as she forces herself to perform the family chores. A child watches and learns. Babies may come quickly—a new brother or a new sister—and just as quickly depart in death. As the preschool child begins to think about the possibility of his own nonbeing, he tends to anticipate his death in these ways that he has learned (Gartley and Bernasconi, 1967). He asks questions about death based on his own experience. When he dies, will he look like the squashed squirrel? He has learned that dead people are buried in the ground, but will he be able to breathe, and will he have anyone to talk to when he is under the earth? He has watched many movie actors agonize in their last gory minutes on the screen, so he ponders whether death will be painful for him also. Those dead soldiers whom he watched on the television news were disfigured; will he also be mutilated and bleeding when he dies? Many preschool children will hesitate to ask these questions directly, but they will all wonder and worry, and they will all fear.

For many children of this preschool age, it is comforting to have death described as a form of sleep, a sleep where they can be secure in the love of those around them. Some children, however, will fear to go to sleep, lest they stay in a death sleep and never wake up again. Where it is appropriate, the preschool child can be told that death is a sleep in the arms of God and that he will awaken in the happiness of heaven, where his parents and his family will eventually rejoin him. Parents, treating personnel and clergy must be aware that most young children are not really pleased to go to heaven because this journey means a separation from their parents and family. The youngster does not want to leave home because he prefers being with his mother, father and family. He asks now whether they are sending him away to heaven because they do not want him. In answer, the dying child can reasonably be told that his parents do not want him to go and and will miss him very much. The dying child and his parents can feel sad together because they are going to be separated. They can comfort one another and recognize again how much they care for each other. The parents may wish to emphasize that this separation, painful as it is for everyone in the family, is only temporary, if indeed they do have such religious beliefs. The innocence and the readiness of the preschool child to believe these concepts make the situation easier. Since the four- or five-year-old child has no definite concept of time, he may think that the separation of death will be merely an overnight sleep with the assuredness of parental love when he awakens. With this support and understanding, the preschool child can die comfortably, secure in the certain knowledge that Mommy and Daddy will never leave him. They will always be with him, on earth or in heaven. With the assuredness that his parents accept him, good as he is and naughty as he may sometimes be, the preschool child can pass through the final stages of life and tolerate the discomfort of death.

He can sleep in peace.

Chapter Three

THE DYING GRADE SCHOOL CHILD

*If I should die
before I wake,
I pray the Lord
my soul to take.*

During the grade school years, the growing child gradually moves out from the protection and security of his home. In this maturation period from five to ten years of age, the youngster begins to take his place as a meaningful member of his community and his culture.

The most obvious and important outward manifestation of this growth move away from the family into society is the fact that the child now goes to school. When he first attends kindergarten or first grade, the youngster tends to be as dependent on his teacher as he has been on his parents up to this time. He looks to his teacher for direction, support and approval in whatever he does, and he seeks comfort, inspiration and security from her. Over the next two or three years, however, the child's way of relating in school begins to change. While the second- or third-grade child is still very responsive to his teacher, he is now starting to respond just as much to the ideas, the way of behavior and the goals that are important to the other children in his class. To an increasing extent, he does things now because his school peers approve. While he still learns from his teacher's example and direction, he may be equally influenced by the attitude and the responses of the boys and girls in his class. During the grade school years, the maturing child develops both intellectually and emotionally as part of a peer group.

As he grows older, the grade school child plays with friends farther and farther away from home. By age nine or ten, many youngsters spend most of their daytime hours away from the security of home and family. If the grade school child has a bicycle, his cycling can range over greater distances. He begins to be more involved in team sports, and his team now is no longer his family group but is an association of children his own age in his own community. He is learning now not only the rules of his small family circle but also the expectations of his school class, his baseball team, his football team, the Boy Scouts or the Young Pioneers. With his friends, he chants, "Simon Says," and plays by the rules of the game. She asks, "Mother, may I?" of her fellow playmates and does what the game demands. The grade school girl skips her hours away to the rhythm chanted by other girls her age. Her play is often minutely directed by rules set down by her peer group. The grade school child is now a member of both his family and of his society.

During the grade school years, the child learns a community awareness, but the impact of this social identify varies between cultures. By age ten, in the Socialist societies, the grade school child has developed a very strong community sensitivity that is well integrated with his total personality. The Soviet youngster appreciates at an early age the importance of community responsibility, community support and community identity. American youngsters are encouraged more to develop their own individuality with less awareness of peer group or social responsibility.

In every culture, society begins to demand increasing self-control and cooperation from the grade school child. His school teachers expect him to stay still and seated in his chair for longer and longer periods as he grows older. While he moves from kindergarten through the various school grades, he learns to behave and respond according to the school schedule and regulations. (Sometimes the grade school child is placed in a very difficult situation if the rules of his school culture are in conflict with his family standards.) School and the community insist that the grade school child devote an increasing amount of energy to intellectual growth and mastery as he becomes older. In the early grade school years, the young child tends to resist these controls and this academic harnessing of his energy. However, at some time during the grade school period, most children find that they are able to master things intellectually and they can solve problems better by thinking than by action. This newfound ability, this new sense of power, is likely to be very exciting to the growing child who realizes that he has this ability now to think and plan for himself. School learning may become a pleasure rather than a chore, something the child enjoys doing rather than something he has to do. If studying and school learning do not become tasks the child wants to do himself by the time the youngster has passed through the grade school years, he will find it very difficult to learn efficiently at the high school level. In adolescence, he is liable to be increasingly stunted intellectually and more frustrated emotionally.

With this rapidly developing ability to learn and master information from the world around him, the grade school child finds himself increasingly bombarded by a wide range of new ideas and opinions. In his reading, his television viewing and his discussion with peers and adults, he is under all kinds of pressures by people whose attitudes and ideas are different from those he learned in the security of his family. As these new opportunities for knowledge open up to him, the grade school child increasingly has to choose and decide. He has already learned how his family feels and thinks, but now he is being faced with different and contrasting opinions. To an increasing extent the grade school child has to make up his own mind.

No matter what he does or learns during these grade school years, the preadolescent child still tends to return home when it is all over. Even though he is happy in his play with the children of his own age, inevitably the play comes to an end, and the child goes back to the comfort and security of his family. When he has listened to and learned from the opinions and the attitudes of teachers, schoolmates, television performers and newspaper headlines, the grade school child still comes back to his parents and his family for a firmer, final opinion. During these grade school years, the child is moving away from home intellectually and emotionally, but he continues to depend on his home and his family for his basic security and continued stability.

During these early school years, the growing youngster is developing a stronger and more stable awareness of himself as an individual and as a unique, separate person with his own special meaning and purpose. In response to the continued pressure of family and community expectations, the little boy is more firmly directed in the path of future manhood, and the little girl is led towards deepening femininity. Boys tend to play with boys and girls with girls so that boys learn to treat girls differently, and girls deal with boys in a fashion different than they do with girls. The cross sex roles complement and reinforce each other. While "boys will be boys" and constitutional factors are very important, the youngster's secure masculine identification is largely dependent on the support and example of father, teachers and other boys and men during the child's formative grade school years. In a similar fashion, the girl in the family learns from her mother, her aunts, her grandmother, the lady next door and every woman with whom she has contact how to be a young woman.

Gradually dependence on the family changes as the grade school child grows. While the kindergarten youngster must constantly refer back to his parents for direction, during the next four or five grade school years, the child will develop an increasing ability to carry his parental standards and ideas with him. By age ten, he should no longer have to ask his parents constantly for direction because he can carry their attitudes with him as part of his own personality. By then he will have internalized the family way of life and identified with his own family standards.

In the year or two just before puberty, the young boy or girl frequently develops a closer relationship with someone his own or her own age and sex. The ten-year-old boy begins to have a close "buddy," the nine-year-old girl has her own special girl friend. These two friends understand each other, trust one another and have very warm and caring feelings for each other. Typically in these close relationships, these children are very sensitive to the feelings of each other in a supportive, growth-encouraging fashion. When this buddy relationship is looked at closely, it will be seen that these two grade school boys care for each other in many ways as if they were parents to one another. The young boy looks at his problems and makes his decisions with the help of his buddy and uses his close friend in the same way that he has been using his parents in the past. For his part, the buddy often acts and talks according to the standards of his own parents. The grade school girl works out her private problems in the same kind of confidential talks with her special girl friend and very much in the same fashion that she used to do with her parents. This close one-to-one relationship, where two grade school children act as mutual parent-confidants to each other, seems to be an important preliminary stage to the youngster's future emancipation from his own parents and family during the adolescent decade. At this late grade school period, the child is still maintaining the parental standards, but these standards, these patterns of behavior, this support, are provided in part by the parents and often, in a parenting role, also by a very close friend with whom the child can identify and towards whom the youngster can also act as a parent.

With each growth step that the grade school child makes towards greater independence and self-sufficiency, he is faced also with a greater appreciation that separateness brings also vulnerability and that self-assertion invites counterchallenge and possible defeat. The grade school child is very aware that he is only a small human being in a very large world. This knowledge, this sense of insignificance, is sometimes very uncomfortable to the growing youngster. The child normally handles these feelings of inadequacy by denial and by emotional reaction formation. At times the grade school child overreacts to his awkward awareness that he is rather small, insignificant and weak by being the pompous braggart. He is "the king of the castle." With magnificent showmanship and apparent total disregard for danger, he cycles around the block with no hands on the bicycle. He balances out on the quivering tree limb and gains great pleasure from the dismay of his parents. In the same way, the grade school girl slides gaily across the ice; no one can say that she is afraid. Thin ice? She is not scared, of course. Especially in the preadolescent years, the grade school child acts as if he is showing to himself and to others that he is not afraid of the world around him. When he is pushing himself to achieve and sometimes to overachieve in this fashion, he is also developing increasing mastery of his environment and his body. As more of an individual now, he is separate and, inevitably, more isolated. He is alive, and he now knows this with great intensity. But, he now senses he can become not alive. He can die. He fears dying.

"If I should die before I wake"

While the grade school child is developing this more definite, integrated awareness of his own individuality and his definite Self, he is also becoming more able to think and feel outside the boundaries of this Self. As he becomes more sure of his own well-defined identity, his own body boundaries and his physical limits, he is starting to think beyond these boundaries. During the grade school years, the growing child is developing an increasing ability to fantasy and to daydream. With the development of imagination, the grade school child now has a much wider range of emotional and intellectual mastery. The grade school years are the time of the handsome prince and the fairy princess. This is the age of Paul Bunyan and Babe, of George Washington and his cherry tree. She is a queen. He is an astronaut. She is a movie star, and he an international rock hero. As he enjoys the strength that he is developing in his muscles, he can daydream privately that someday he might be a prizefighter—the cheers, the noise, the rewards—and how proud his mother and father will be of him. As the grade school girl admires the smoothness of her hair in the mirror, she can also see in her mind that beautiful diamond-studded crown on top of those curls. She can hear the coronation bells, and she smiles as she imagines her parents' pleasure.

As the grade school child becomes more aware of his independent role in society, he also is developing a new ability to understand that there has been a past before him and that there may be a future yet to come. He is now understanding the significance of time continuity. He is developing an ability to imagine in the future things pleasant and unpleasant. From the family photographs, he learns that the old people around him were once young and gay. In their wrinkled faces, he can see the faded remnants of former youth and vigor. From the pictures, he sees that Daddy was once a baby and then a boy like him but now he is bald and fat and tires easily. She laughs when her relatives tell about all the things Mommy did when she was a little girl, but she notices now that Mommy's hair is gray and her arthritis bothers her at night. The grade school child begins to understand more and more that he himself may live and grow or he may die and disappear. He is now developing the ability to imagine himself well and healthy or sick and dying. He now can fantasy death, and he is beginning to grasp the idea that he, as an individual, may die. In this way, the grade school child is developing the ability to understand the diagnosis and the prognosis (Solnit and Green, 1963; Menig-Peterson and McCabe, 1978).

As part of this normal emotional and intellectual growth, the grade school child starts to wonder about an alternative to death—a hereafter, a heaven, a paradise or even a hell (Schilder and Wechsler, 1934). Often, with the encouragement and teaching of the religion of his family and his culture, he reassures himself that this newly developed individuality will somehow continue to exist. He would like to believe that even if this present individuality is changed in some way, possibly by a process called death, there will still continue to be a "me" somewhere, there will still be a post-self (Shneidman, 1964; Gartley and Bernasconi, 1967). In the child's mind, even a continued existence in the torments of hell may be preferable to the horrible, formless anxiety of not existing at all. Now that the child is sure of his existence, he wants it to continue, and heaven, of course, is by far the best solution.

"I pray the Lord my soul to take"

As the grade school child has been growing older and more mature, he has been learning the rules of his community. From his parents and family, he has been taught through day-to-day experience what is expected of him, what behavior is rewarded and what behavior is punished. When he enters school first, he judges what he does and what others do by the standards he has learned within his family. At the kindergarten age level, the young child behaves in the way his parents want. His young conscience is molded by the expectations and examples of his mother, father and family. In the grade school years, the growing youngster strengthens this identification with the parents. The young boy imitates his father more and more, and the young girl models herself after her mother. During this time, from five to ten years of age, the growing youngster begins to understand that both his parents are human beings with human feelings and fallibilities. He becomes more aware that they can be wrong and sometimes they are weak. He comes to realize that his parents can be enfeebled by time and destroyed by death. In the past, he has depended on them for protection and guidance, but gradually, the grade school child begins to seek other heroes to worship and other authorities to provide protection.

In a stable community, the grade school youngster believes that representatives of society—the policemen, the firemen and the school principal—are dependable sources of strength and safety. For even greater security, he thinks he can depend on the leaders of his nation and his race; he believes in the president; he follows the guidance of the pope; he learns the words of his ethnic leader. The grade school years are the time in life when the child begins to grope for someone and something to believe in and to worship—a deity, a cause, a purpose—Jesus, Buddha, Muhammad or even Lenin. As he learns his own human frailty and the frailty of those around him, the grade school child still needs to have faith in something and someone more powerful than his own uncertain strengths or his parents' increasing vulnerability.

With the rules of God, society, his family and his peer group, the young child during the grade school years likes to organize his universe methodically: "One potato, two potato, three potato, four. Five potato, six potato, seven potato, more!" and inevitably, "out!" To help him adapt to his role in the world, the grade school child prefers to arrange things and events in a neat, predictable fashion. Thus, everything is seen as having a cause and a purpose and so becomes much more predictable. Every act must have a punishment or a reward. Conversely, to the grade school child, every punishment must have been produced by some bad act or nasty thought. Extremely bad thoughts or wicked actions, of course, must bring the most dire punishments—an eye for an eye and a tooth for a tooth. The grade school child is likely to feel that he is being punished when he is faced with the prospect of his own dying. By the standards of his newly developed conscience, he views death as a penalty that must have been brought on him by something he said or did, by someone powerful like a parent or God. He is still small and vulnerable, so he needs the support of his family and his God to direct his life and to make his decisions, but he feels that some parent-person or a God somewhere has judged him to be wicked, and so he has been punished. How else can he understand his death? How can he deal with dying?

The grade school child must be assured in every way, by his parents' actions and words, that he is not being punished or sent away by them. He may not easily agree when he is told that he will be happier in heaven because he realizes that in heaven he will be separated from his parents. He does not want to leave his family and his friends, especially now that he is enjoying himself. The grade school child will feel more accepted if he is told that his father and mother do not wish to see him go. He and his parents then can have this common bond of sadness at the separation that will come when the child dies. They may agree together that "it is God's will," and they can help each other accept this destiny. In the devoutly religious family, God can always take the full responsibility for the child's dying, since death is beyond human understanding and control. God is well able to take the burden of this decision and face the questions, the anger and the anxieties.

As the grade school child grows, he learns about the meaning of physical death (Klingberg, 1957). In movies and on television, he sees people dying, he witnesses their death throes. On the news and in the papers, he is taught that people are maimed and killed, and he sees also that these people have families. As he watches, he can see so easily that these men who are dying are just like his daddy. They must be fathers too. To an increasing extent, the grade school child learns that the process of death is not reversible. He finds that Snow White was only a very happy story, and a kiss does not awaken you when you are dead. He learns that death will not go away. Once it seemed that death occurred mostly to old people, but the grade school youngster is beginning to learn that this is not an infallible rule. He comes to realize that sometimes death takes even the very young. Death strikes down the boy in the next class or the girl who lives down the block. Death takes away a cousin or the little baby they waited for so long. The grade school child worries and wonders. He still is likely to think that death occurs more often with a loud noise, a splash or a bang, but he is learning, and learning uncomfortably, that sometimes death happens quietly and stealthily. By the preadolescent years, most grade school children are well versed in the significance of the common diagnoses. From television shows or from newspaper articles, he has come to understand what leukemia is and does. From his family's responses, he knows how people react when cancer is mentioned (Le Shan, 1961). In the books he reads and enjoys, the heroes and heroines are sometimes injured and killed. When Beth dies, the young reader cries to herself, not only because she feels sadness at the loss of the little heroine, but also because she can now imagine herself in the same situation. She can die, and she knows it.

With his more mature sense of individuality and his recognition of human vulnerability, the grade school child appreciates more clearly what death can now mean to him. These emotions and ideas are much too disturbing. So, like human beings at every other age level, the grade school child must shut out these feelings, this awareness that somehow he could cease to exist. He knows somehow he will die, but he still believes that he will be secure and protected. The grade school child still depends on parental authorities—God, doctors, teachers—for his final protection, so he is still certain that he will be protected somehow.

When the grade school child is hospitalized, he is separated usually from his family on whom he depends for his comfort, security and guidance. Most grade school children are scared, lonely and sad when first they are sent to a hospital, but usually they manage to adapt and to cope. The youngster is afraid of this new and unknown situation—the antiseptic hospital rooms with the strange smells, the scrubbed, uniformed nurses who rustle in their starched primness and the physicians with their unintelligible words. The child is scared, sometimes desperately scared, but usually he controls himself. He is proud, and he knows that other people are watching him. The grade school child can be very lonely away from his parents. He misses them desperately. He is angry, frustrated and very worried because this place is so strange. The child's anger and resentment may be expressed towards the treatment team, and the youngster may refuse to cooperate. If the situation is too demanding and stressful, the hospitalized grade school child may become withdrawn or obviously overwhelmed. To help the grade school youngster deal with this separation, it is useful to allow the parents to be with him as much as possible, since he still needs his parents as allies in dealing with the problems he now faces in this strange hospital environment.

In the deepening shadows and the loneliness of the hospital evening, the kindergarten child especially needs the security of mother's warmth sitting by his bedside. As he waits for those attendants to take him to that dreaded operating theater, the eight-year-old boy can feel much safer with father's hand in his. When he feels strange and alone in the hospital, the grade school child can be greatly reassured by the visits of his schoolmates. The grade school youngster does not need his parents to tell him what to do, but he needs their support to help him accomplish what he has decided to do himself and what he must do.

Just as the grade school child learns from the other children in his school class, so is he taught by his fellow patients. Very quickly the young child learns the hospital routines and the significance of the different procedures. If a hospital unit is devoted to the treatment of one specific disease, the grade school child recognizes within a matter of hours the significance of his situation. He rapidly learns the different communications on the unit. With little coaching, he discovers that extra visiting privileges mean that death is fast approaching. He soon notices that patients nearing death somehow are moved nearer and nearer the door. He cannot fail to see that the treating staff seem to pass more hurriedly by the patients who are not responding to treatment. The doctor has a special face, a fixed tone of voice and a hearty manner whenever "the case" begins to do badly.

Though the grade school patient quickly learns the fears and anxieties of his hospital unit, he also becomes part of the group denial process that typically exists on such a unit. With the support and agreement of the patients and staff, he will find that he does not notice when the bed pattern is changed. He will learn not to become disturbed when a member of the patient group disappears and never returns (Spinetta, 1974). Each young patient works with the other patients to maintain this denial and to preserve this necessary facade. With this kind of group support and group defense, the grade school child is usually able to cooperate in his treatment as part of the peer age patient group. Unfortunately, group denial sometimes collapses under the pressure of group anxieties, and suddenly, and sometimes unexpectedly, a whole hospital ward can become deeply and disturbingly anxious and upset. At these times especially, the grade school child should be encouraged to use his parents and the treatment staff for firm guidance and strong support.

Because the grade school youngster wants to feel in control of his own situation, he often takes great pleasure in giving out the medications and usually is much happier when he is involved in his own treatment procedures, even though the treatment may be painful. With his age-appropriate need for neatness and organization, the grade school child can be the one to tell the nurse when his medication is due or even when his dosage is incorrect. He can very usefully help organize other patients, with pride he can push wheelchairs, with responsibility he can run errands—in short, he benefits from being part of the hospital family.

The growing youngster, age six to ten, cannot avoid being aware at some level of what is happening to himself. He can, however, share his burden and use support. The experience of dying can be the deepest and warmest interaction that the grade school child will ever have had with his family. He is able to turn to them for the most meaningful security and for the most profound comfort, and he and his parents can share their very deep bond of love and understanding. When the grade school child asks about his situation, he should be told the truth in terms that he can understand. When he asks about his diagnosis, he can be given a very simple, basic explanation. If he asks about the prognosis for his disease, he should be given a firm but general answer. Early in the illness, the grade school child can be told quite honestly that no physician can tell how long any illness might last, because each individual and each illness is different. Wherever possible, the youngster should be given hope, realistic hope. The treatment procedures should be explained to him in advance so that he can cooperate in any way possible. When eventually death is near and inevitable, the child's questions should be responded to truthfully. At this age, the grade school child has the emotional ability to face the prospect of dying and to reach out to his parents and to his family for comfort and understanding.

> *Yea, though I walk through the valley of*
> *the shadow of death, I will fear no evil:*
> *For Thou art with me; Thy rod and Thy*
> *staff they comfort me.*
>
> ***Psalm 23***

This verse was written by a believer, but these words could have been said by a grade school child. A child of this age believes in parents, family and God. The grade school child knows that death means a final separation from this life. He appreciates now what he will miss when he dies, and he must mourn this loss as he leaves. He is liable to be sad and bitter because he does not want to go. He is lonely because he is traveling this journey alone. As he is dying, the grade school child can use his parents, his family, his buddy or best friend and his classmates to help him live through this final experience. The grade school child can always use the support and the understanding of those whom he trusts and, in his own way, can give support and comfort. In his final days and hours, the grade school child should live through the experience of death in the comfort of his family and friends.

Chapter Four

THE DYING ADOLESCENT

In response to the pressures of emotional growth, of constitutional biological changes and of family and social expectations, the growing child strives to achieve adult independence and competency during the second decade of life. The maturation task of the normal teenager is to become more separate emotionally and intellectually from his parents and family, to develop and test his own ideas and opinions and to establish himself as a self-sufficient adult, mature and effective in his own culture.

Early Adolescence

Across the world, the onset of puberty and the beginning of adolescence is coming sooner. In all cultures, however, adolescent growth of the girl begins one to two years before that of the boy. In the industrial nations, the early years of adolescence for boys come in the age period from ten to fourteen and, during this time, the developing teenager typically moves out socially from the protection of parents and family. In this growth away from the family, the young teenager usually becomes part of a same sex peer group. Though the young adolescent may seem to be interested in this social group of young people for their own sake, on closer evaluation it can be recognized that the interest of the teenager is almost completely self-centered and narcissistic at this stage of development. The young adolescent associates with other young people whose main qualification for his friendship is that they act and think as he does. The young teenage boy will protest very honestly that he must be loyal to his friends because "we all think alike." The young adolescent girl will strenuously refuse to change the way she dresses because "all the girls do it," and they certainly do at this stage of adolescence. In the junior high schools, the teenagers tend to dress alike, think alike, feel alike and react alike—giving each other strength and support as they loosen family ties.

At this age period, most normal teenagers resist parental demands that would in any way make them different from the peer group. The young teenager depends on his gang, his crowd, his group, to help him plan and decide. He needs the strength of the guys, and she needs the support of the girls to know how to react in these early teenage years. They hesitate to make decisions their peers might not make. Though he prides himself that he has become so independent, the young teenager has merely given up parental direction for group direction. Teenagers emancipate themselves from the family more comfortably and effectively if they are sure of the continued security of the family. Though they are independent, they always have a home and a family to go back to when they need security and stable standards. When the young adolescent is faced with his own dying, however, his peer group tends to fail him at that time, and he has to depend on himself and his family.

Some teenagers find it more difficult to separate easily from their parents. Certain young adolescents never emancipate themselves and grow from dependent childhood to dependent adulthood. Other adolescents have to emancipate themselves too abruptly because they fear their own need to be dependent. If the adolescent and his family have had an angry, rejecting or unstable relationship when the teenager was younger, the young person may find it only too easy to sever his family ties abruptly. Emotionally he may cut himself totally adrift from his family, only to find that he cannot cope with the stresses of adolescenthood on his own. Other teenagers who have had an unusually close relationship with parents and family may find it difficult to change these very rewarding family relationships. They are liable to feel a strong need to stay small and dependent, and since they enjoyed the pleasures of being small and protected, they find themselves hesitant to be really independent. In order to force their own independence, these more dependent adolescents are prone to emancipate themselves abruptly, drastically and sometimes painfully from their families. Both the teenager who has felt deprived and rejected by his parents and the adolescent who has been unusually close to his family are likely to emancipate themselves too completely and too quickly from their families and are apt then to find themselves more dependent on their peer group for support and direction. Since they have so completely separated from their parents, these teenagers sometimes have no emotional option but to allow their lives to be dictated by the attitudes of the group. The adolescent who is absolutely gang-oriented will find it very difficult then to develop his own individual ideas and opinions, and his continued emotional growth will become increasingly stunted. If he is faced then with the reality of death, he is likely to have only his gang, his peer group, to call on for support and understanding, and they may be of little help.

As the teenager grows away emotionally from his parents, he typically goes through a phase when he also dissociates himself from their religion and their culture. To emphasize his independence, the young adolescent frequently refuses to go to church or synagogue and may loudly proclaim his absolute disagreement with the established social and legal system. In an atheistic society, the adolescent may rebel against parental standards by insisting on going to church. To resist this regressive pull that he feels back to the protection and warmth of childhood, the teenager is prone to react strenuously against anything parental.

Usually the growing adolescent shows this emancipation rebellion in more socially tolerable ways. The young teenager will wear clothes and hairstyles that are different from those of the parents' generation. If parents had short hair, teenagers tend to insist on long hair and pendulous bangs. Then those same teenagers themselves become parents and, a generation later with their hair still long, find that their children insist on having shorter hair. Where mother wears jeans, the teenage girl may want to wear dresses. In these ways, teenagers emphasize that they are separate, different and independent from their parents. If these behavior patterns are not carried to extremes and if parents do not become overly controlling, this behavior allows the adolescent to test out ideas and attitudes that are a change from those which he has learned within the family. He and his parents sometimes discover, often to the surprise of everyone concerned, that some of these different ideas are really very reasonable and should be adopted by everyone. The teenager then may have the very beneficial growth experience of teaching his parents. At the same time, however, parents need to allow adolescents to be different and should permit generational differences. When parents themselves become adolescent, they make it extremely difficult for the teenager to be truly independent.

Although the young adolescent is emancipating himself from his parents and family, this emotional growth and separation is not without pain or guilt to the teenager. Though the young man may loudly proclaim that he rejects every family standard, he developed his basic personality strengths during the first decade of life when he was a family member, and whether he likes it or not, the adolescent will always measure the actions and behavior of himself and his society against those principles he learned in his early family years. The guidelines he will always have for his conscience are those which were established in the family when he was a preadolescent child. If the teenager has had any meaningful, stable relationship within his family during his first decade of life, he will never be able to undo completely those early patterns of behavior just because he is becoming emancipated. During the adolescent years, the young adolescent often feels vaguely unworthy and uneasily guilty because he knows that he is rejecting parental control and going against some of the parental standards. He may not change his behavior, but the fact that he is rejecting these usually bothers him. When he challenges his parents, even as part of a normal, healthy adolescent emancipation, the teenager still feels guilty and tends to expect that in some way he will be punished.

Most deaths in adolescents are due to accidents and trauma. Teenagers die most often because they are breaking the rules of parents and society. Adolescent accidental deaths occur most frequently due to automobile speeding, alcohol and the use of drugs—frequently in combination. These accidents are much more likely to occur when the teenager is experimenting and exploring, frequently in opposition to the rules and the standards of his family and culture. In the developing nations, the toll of adolescent deaths is rising rapidly because adolescent experimentation is occurring in a society that is also experimenting.

Because the young adolescent already has this tendency to feel guilty as he separates emotionally from his parents, a fatal accident or death-producing illness is frequently seen as a confirmation that he has been bad. The teenager senses that what is happening to him is a well-merited punishment. Since the normal, growing adolescent naturally tests and breaks many rules of his culture and his family, he can very easily see his dying and his death as a punishment for the transgressions that he has committed. Punishment as dreadful as a sentence of death can only occur to someone who has been very bad; the young dying adolescent is likely to feel guilty and depressed due to what is happening to him. He is likely to blame himself and often with good reason.

This death sentence, this overwhelming punishment, will appear to the teenager to be the kind of penalty that only an unforgiving, brutal parental authority could mete out. The growing adolescent will then react with fear to any authority figure that seems to punish in this absolute fashion. How can he really believe in parents, in his society or in a God that treats him this way or allows him to die at this young age? He is likely to feel that he has tried to be independent, but his presumptuousness, his self-assertiveness, has been overwhelmingly smashed by this sentence of death. He reached for the flame of independence, and the gods struck him down for his temerity. In his fear and his guilt, the young dying adolescent may feel that he has no one outside his peer group to whom he can turn for support or understanding.

The young dying teenager is likely to feel very bitter and angry at the death penalty that is being exacted. The anger that the dying teenager feels towards his parents, his family and his god may make him feel even more sinful and guilty. He feels even worse emotionally because he knows he is bitter and resentful towards those people for whom he does care deeply. He is angry at himself for the way he feels, since he recognizes that these strong feelings show how much he cares for his family and how he still, in many ways, is dependent on them, even when everyone thinks he is independent. How dare he allow himself to care this much? How dare they allow him still to be dependent? His resentment deepens his guilt and is liable to accentuate his depressive feelings. The young teenager may face death lonely and alone. He feels rejected by punitive parents, by a resentful society and by an unforgiving deity (Murphy, 1978).

The young adolescent who is dying is liable to find himself rejected by his gang. His teenage friends often pull back from him when they sense that he is dying. These young men and women are themselves working very hard to establish their own self-sufficiency and independence. They are building their own strengths and solidifying their own opinions. Death, and especially the death of a friend and someone their own age, faces them too directly with their own vulnerability and fragility. Young adolescents find it very difficult to deal with human frailty and withdraw from anyone, especially another teenager, who faces them too openly with the possibility of death. They are usually very uncomfortable in the presence of the maimed or the disfigured and may be too uneasy to face someone their own age who is dying (Chodoff, 1959; Hankoff, 1975; LePontois, 1975).

The young adolescent who is facing death is often very lonely. He feels that somehow his parents have failed him, and he is liable to find himself isolated by his peers. He treasures his new independence, but finds himself in enforced dependency due to his illness. He cannot look back on a full life to support his sense of successful independence, and now illness takes away what little independence he had. He recognizes that the approach of death is the harbinger of a final, total passivity and frequently struggles against this dependent role. The fatally ill young adolescent may insist on continuing to do things for himself, so he overtaxes his strength. To bolster his self-esteem and to deny his own sense of mutilation, he may ridicule other patients who are handicapped. The young adolescent has to reemphasize to himself that he is self-sufficient and independent, so he is apt to tell his friends and his family that they should not bother coming to see him. He may airily dismiss his illness as "no big thing." If the young adolescent turns to his parents for support, understanding and comfort, he is likely to feel that somehow he is surrendering. As a reaction to these feelings, the young teenager is apt to reject his parents, his family and the adult members of his treatment team, not because he does not desperately want their understanding and support, but in reality because he longs so much for their warmth and caring that he cannot allow himself to admit these feelings. The young adolescent must keep his pride.

The dying teenage girl may wish so intensely to be cared for and protected that she dreads losing control over herself (Abrams, 1966). Although she longs for understanding, she fears the loss of her new independence, so she has to push people away. Gifts may be tossed away unopened; she cannot admit to anyone that she wants this kind of attention. Letters may be left lying around unread to show to everyone how self-sufficient she really is. The proud young teenager may long to open the gifts or read the letters, but her pride may prevent her from showing too openly that she cares. Parents, family and caring professionals need to give and to care without asking for acknowledgement so that the adolescent can receive without fuss, without shame and without feeling inadequate or dependent.

As the natural process of dying evolves, the fatally ill adolescent may become so weak physically that he can allow himself to be cared for and loved without feeling that he has voluntarily surrendered. He can now tell himself that he has no option, and he can say that, once he gets stronger, he will again assume full control and get rid of all these fussy people. At this stage of illness, the young adolescent may still be unable to ask directly for mothering or fathering, but he is likely to accept, without too much resistance, the attention that his parents and family have been wanting to give him all along. Without asking, without recrimination, relatives should continue to be warm, kind and comforting, and as the young teenager approaches death, he may be able to accept their caring without losing his dignity. As he approaches his final weeks and days, the dying young teenager will tolerate visits where he would not have endured the presence of his family before. He may accept gifts of books, fruit or candy, whereas weeks or even days earlier these signs of family concern would have been immediately consigned to the garbage. In his last days and hours, the young adolescent may eventually respond as a very young child and allow himself to be comforted and even babied, as long as no one threatens his self-respect by pointing out to him that he is being treated as a child. Even though emotionally he is no longer functioning as a proud, emancipated teenager, he must always be respected as a self-sufficient young adult. The dying adolescent, age ten to fourteen or fifteen years, is likely to allow himself to be a child in the bosom of his family as death grows near, as long as he is respected.

In this early half of the adolescent decade when the normal teenager is emancipating himself from the family, the youngster is acutely sensitive and perceptive to the new and intense feelings he is experiencing. In many ways, the young teenager is closer to a childlike innocence and sensitivity that he had been since his preschool years and possibly will ever be again. He has fewer emotional barriers and is more able to experience his perceptions both of his inner world and of the world around him. The young adolescent is supremely able to feel, to live and to be. He is alive with a total vibrancy and an all-encompassing passion. He can feel with all his senses. He can float in a sunset. He can wallow in the scents of the afternoon flowers. He can conjure up a tune and play it to the melody of the waving grass. If an adolescent is very lucky, when he grows up, he does not lose this sensitivity.

The young adolescent, who is so able to experience life, can also experience death to its fullest. He can echo the words of Keats—

> *. . . and for many a time*
> *I have been half in love with easeful Death,*
> *Call'd him soft names in many a mused rhyme,*
> *To take into the air my quiet breath;*
> *Now more than ever seems it rich to die,*
> *to cease upon the midnight with no pain,*
> *While thou art pouring forth thy soul abroad*
> *In such an ecstasy!*

The adolescent wants to live and live totally. Death fascinates him because it is one of the deeper experiences of life, and most normal adolescents toy at some time with the possibility of dying because they are so interested in living. While the teenager may be fascinated with dying as a part of living, he certainly does not want to stop existing. He is vibrantly aware of his being, but he is also deeply sensitive to the meaning of nonbeing. He knows the real richness of life so why should anyone kill? Why should anyone die? Why should there be wars? Why death—to anyone, to me? If the adolescent is dying, the teenager can recognize that death is taking life from him just when he has come to realize the full possibilities of his existence.

Very understandably, the young adolescent who is dying feels deeply deprived and very resentful, but he has no place to direct this anger. There is no one whom he can ask, "Why me?" or "Who is to blame?" The young teenager feels that he has been taken to the mountain top and shown the promised land only to be told that this promise and this land are not for him. Since the young teenager can feel the meaning and the reality of life so deeply, he can also appreciate how much he will lose now that he is dying. As Hamovitch (1964) points out, the bitterness of the young adolescent who is dying probably causes more problems to his family and to the treating staff than the reactions of any other fatally ill patient group. It is not fair!

Death is a task that the young teenager has to face alone. The family and the caring team must continue to be supportive as he carries his burden by himself. Even though the young adolescent is irritable and bitter, his family and those who care for him should continue to show by their actions and their words that they still love him. The proud young adolescent will find it very difficult to accept any relative who expresses these feelings to him too directly, but the visits and the caring give this message over and over again in a way that the adolescent may be able to tolerate without losing face and without giving up his pride. Even though the teenager may protest that letters do not interest him, that flowers are a waste of money and that candy nauseates him, all these signs of attention help the young adolescent appreciate that he is not really alone, no matter what he thinks or what he feels. While the young dying adolescent may be much too proud or too independent ever to be able to express thanks, this understanding support from his family and the treatment staff make the loneliness of his dying more bearable and the bitterness at giving up life less acute.

Midadolescence

By midadolescence, the growing adolescent has developed more secure self-confidence and a greater independence. He still is trying out his own opinions and ideas, but more and more, he is comfortable in who he is and what he wants. Slowly, and still sometimes painfully, he develops self-control, self-confidence and self-goals in directions that are now not always the same as his peer group's. To an increasing extent, the fifteen- and sixteen-year-old boy is taking pride in himself as an adult individual and not merely as someone who is part of a teenage group. By this age, the young girl now enjoys her own personal abilities and is less dependent on what her gang does or wants. She now values her own opinions and expresses attitudes that are more personal and less an echo of what her friends think. By midadolescence, the adolescent boy takes pleasure in the things he can do himself and in the individual way that he can do them. As he looks in the mirror, he likes what he sees because it is himself. While he understands that he is not physically perfect, he does find himself attractive and pleasing. When he looks at his reflection, he wrinkles up his chin to display that new growth of tender beard. The adolescent girl turns sideways to see whether she would look even better if she held herself in a little more here—or there—even there. She brushes out her eyelashes to give them that coquettish curl. By midadolescence, the maturing teenager is much more sure of his own adult, independent individuality.

To this newly competent adolescent, fifteen or sixteen years old, death promises only a defeat (Koocher, 1976). To the young teenage girl who has just begun to enjoy her own maturing feminity, death brings a withering and then a destruction. The sixteen-year-old boy who has been taking increasing pride in his masculine strength understands only too well that death will shrink, weaken and eventually stop the power of these muscles forever. The fifteen-year-old girl, who has laughed with lilting joy at her developing feminine roundness and womanly vitality, appreciates very clearly that death will blight her beauty and quench her energy. By the middle adolescent years, the teenager is achieving confidently and is mastering competently. The fifteen- or sixteen-year-old adolescent is enjoying the power, the beauty and the force of sexuality. The adolescent of this age has begun to realize the adult power that comes also with self-control and personal competence. Now, too, the young adolescent can understand the power of death, for death will take all this away. The sixteen-year-old can appreciate the cruel reality of death to the fullest. An adolescent of this age will normally and very understandably react to the prospect of death with anger, bitterness and futile, hopeless rage—rage at the supidity of it all, rage at the waste of this whole process of living and dying, rage at the absolute powerlessness that the teenager now feels in spite of all his newly developed abilities.

As death grows nearer, the disease process may deform before it destroys. A slow death is liable to cause the dying adolescent or young adult a great deal of emotional agony. The young man who was once so active and virile may be maimed and disfigured by an accident that eventually results in his death. Before dying takes its final toll, he will have to face the loss of his attractiveness. Before the metastases finally kill her, the sixteen-year-old girl may have to undergo a deforming operation to slow the cancer spread. Where once she was so proud of her dancing, she sits, a wallflower waiting for her final partner. The adolescent blush of joy may give way to the leukemic bruise. To have known the joy makes the bruise even more painful and less bearable. Because the fifteen-year-old teenager has tasted the pleasures of personal mastery and self-achievement, he feels death to be an even greater deprivation. He is likely to be furious and enraged. In his mind there is never any justification sufficient for what is happening to him. The competent adolescent hates death with the passion of one who knows how to live.

Late Adolescence

In the late adolescent years when the teenager has developed greater self-confidence, he will have much less tendency to reject the care and sympathy of his parents and his family. When the growing young man knows comfortably that he is a competent male, he will have less need to challenge his father. When the adolescent has developed a solid sense of independence and no longer has to fear becoming a dependent little boy again, he can accept his mother's love and even be childlike at times. If the sixteen-year-old young woman is sure of her own feminine attractiveness, she can now more easily accept her father's admiration and her mother's companionship. The more secure the young teenage woman has become in her own sense of womanhood, the more readily will she now be able to accept mothering and caring. The young man who believes he is a man in his own right will not reject the support and the consolation of his own father. Even though he is angry, bitter and furious at his fate, the older adolescent who is dying can more readily accept the understanding and the expressions of love of his parents, his brothers and sisters, and his family as he moves through the process of death.

The older teenager may periodically unload his frustrated rage on his family, but usually he tries to control and direct these feelings elsewhere. However, treatment team members are liable to see periodic explosions of bitterness, anger or fear. A minor change in the treatment routine may precipitate a rage outburst. The nurse's joking remark may provoke an unexpected explosion of anger. The caring team must appreciate that these outbursts are primarily an outward sign of the teenager's inner rage at this situation he now faces. Though they should expect the young man or woman to handle these feelings more appropriately, treatment personnel must understand that such angry eruptions are usually not meant for them personally. It is helpful if the dying adolescent is given some activity into which he can channel his furious rage at what fate is doing to him. It is often useful if the dying teenager can be involved in occupational therapy projects that help him work out his bitterness and rage in a way that does not disrupt his treatment process.

With approaching adulthood, the older adolescent finds, sometimes to his surprise and usually to his great pleasure, that he now has the ability to care deeply for other people. He learns that his greatest emotional joy comes now from caring for and being cared for by other people. He revels in the richness of this newfound relationship ability. The young man has his girlfriend who is the center of his universe. He feels strong and masculine because she cares for him and he cares for her. In all his waking hours and in most of his dreams, she is his life and the purpose of his existence. The older adolescent girl has her special young man whom she adores. She feels feminine and desirable because she loves him and he loves her in return. She learns that the more she gives this person she loves, the greater emotional enrichment she herself receives. By late adolescence, the teenager often learns that life is more important when it is lived for someone else.

As the teenager moves into adulthood, he is developing the deep personal relationships that may endure for the rest of his life, whether he lives seventy days or seventy years. If the young man forms friendships with other teenagers of his own age at this time, these peer relationships are now liable to be lifelong friendships, based on mutual respect for each other. The older adolescent now has learned the lasting value and appreciates the warmth and the strength of his family ties. The young man moves even closer emotionally to his father and finds that he and this older man have a mutually respecting, rewarding partnership. The young lady finds, in an increasingly enriching understanding, that she and her mother can appreciate and care for each other in the deepest, most feminine closeness. Comfortably, but realistically, the young man identifies with the qualities he admires in his father. The young woman deliberately models herself after those feminine attributes she respects and likes in her mother. As the older adolescent increasingly appreciates the relationships he has with his own family, he looks foward to his own life and to the pleasure he hopes to find in a family of his own.

When an older adolescent, on the threshold of adult maturity, is faced with death, he realizes that he will now lose everything that life has come to mean. He has begun to care deeply, and he appreciates he will have to break these emotional bonds when he departs in death. He is increasingly aware of the depth of human understanding and closeness that he can gain in loving relationships, and he is very sensitive to the fact that his death will rob him of this enrichment. He is finding that, as he cares for other people, he himself is growing emotionally and spiritually. He knows that, when death comes to him, he can no longer grow. He recognizes that he is loved by other people who will miss him and whom he will miss.

The young adult does not want to leave life because he has just fully arrived. He has only discovered the range of experiences that life can give. Like all mourners of every age, the older teenager is angry because of what he is going to lose. Sometimes, in spite of themselves, these young adults vent some of this rage on the very people for whom they care. The young man may be deeply distressed and remorseful when he finds himself hurting those people he does not want to leave. The young woman will feel very guilty if she is angry, inwardly or outwardly, towards someone she is going to miss very much when she is dead. Like every mourner, the older adolescent who is dying must reinvest emotionally. He can no longer plan for a full and exciting life ahead. He cannot replace what he is going to lose (Noyes, 1967). Because he is dying, he cannot plan alternative friends or different relationships for those he is about to leave.

As part of the necessary reinvestment process that comes with mourning, the dying adolescent may try to insure that in some fashion he remains as long as possible with his loved ones, in memory or in some more concrete fashion. The young man may fruitfully spend his last hours and days in making arrangements for those family members and friends who will survive him. As the young man of the family, he may try to make sure that his aging parents will have some form of continuing support when he is gone. In this way, he will live in them and somehow his relationship with them will continue. If the older adolescent is married, he may try to live on in a child. The young dying woman may hasten to become pregnant, even at the risk of worsening her physical condition, so that her memory and her being in some way lives on after her. This reinvestment in future things and things that will continue not only helps the older adolescent to reinvest some of his mourning energies, but also allows him to maintain a necessary level of denial. If he believes that he will continue on in memory, in a family project, in a child or even in an annuity, his wonderful, glorious existence is not really completely gone.

As death approaches, the older adolescent—the young adult—often draws closer to his family members. In his last weeks, the young dying adult frequently can allow himself to be cared for and can show his caring more openly. Like any other human being, he will often have to deny the more disturbing uncertainties that he faces in dying, but he can permit himself to care openly and directly.

Adolescents deal with death as they understand it and in their own individual way. No inevitable, preprogrammed responses to dying can be demonstrated in adolescents in any culture. The teenager who is dying should be dealt with truthfully and respectfully no matter what age he may be. If his questions are answered evasively or dishonestly, the adolescent will know that he is being tricked. Most teenagers are very capable of picking up the unspoken communications from family and treating professionals. Where a teenager is not responded to honestly, he will feel, with much justification, that this lack of directness is a sign of disrespect. He is not being treated as an equal, he is being placed in a dependent role. Even though the adolescent may not like the truth, he should always be answered honestly but gently. When he is respected, the adolescent usually can respond with much more self-control and cooperation.

As with patients of any age, the adolescent will usually indicate by his questions what answers he wishes. If the teenager has the emotional need to deny the fact that he is dying, he, like any other patient, should be allowed to maintain his emotional defense. He should never be obliged to face unpleasant and unbearable realities that he is indicating he cannot tolerate. If the adolescent is weeks or months away from death and asks, "I am not going to die, am I?" he is obviously pleading for support for his denial. He must never be told a lie, but he can be answered, "No, you are not going to die right now." This kind of answer allows the teenager to bolster his denial if he has to shut out disturbing feelings. If, on the other hand, the adolescent is emotionally strong enough to deal with his situation more directly, he can follow up this kind of answer by asking a more specific question about his situation. He can then ask, "Well, how long do I have to live?" He has now indicated that he thinks he can tolerate a more direct answer. Even in this situation, he should never be given a reply that absolutely wipes out hope. He can be told realistically, when the average prognosis is for three months survival, "People with an illness like yours may die in three to six months, but sometimes they live much, much longer"—realistic, honest, but hope is still permitted.

The dying adolescent should always be considered a member of the treatment team, undoubtedly, the most important member. The teenager must be told the purpose and the nature of the treatment procedures that are being carried out on his body. He can be informed of the expected benefits and warned of possible unpleasant side effects. Again, the questions the adolescent asks will usually indicate how much knowledge of his situation he can tolerate. There is usually little point in explaining detailed surgical techniques to the teenage patient, but it is often very helpful when he knows that an operation is planned to remove a block in his bowel. He can be warned in advance that a treatment or an operation is likely to have certain effects so that he comes to appreciate that not everything that happens to him occurs by chance or due to some implacable fate. Some teenagers will need to know many more details about their illness and treatment process because this knowledge gives them a greater sense of intellectual control of their situation.

While the treatment team should appreciate and understand the rage, the bitterness and the resentment that the dying teenager feels at his fate, they should never allow this anger to disrupt or prevent necessary therapeutic procedures. Sometimes the dying adolescent poses a very difficult management problem to parents and caring professionals. All dying teenagers deeply resent the fact that they are fated to die. The older adolescent can usually cooperate with the treatment procedures in spite of his resentment. The more mature teenager, who is now really a young man or a young woman, will allow family and caring staff to comfort and care. Sad, but proud, the older adolescent can go to his death, mourned and mourning. The younger adolescent, age ten to fifteen years, may be much too proud and bitter to accept very much comfort or open understanding. Defiant in the face of death, desperately proud and often painfully lonely, the younger adolescent may insist on going through death, fiercely independent to the end.

THE FAMILY OF THE DYING CHILD

When parents first learn that their child is dying, they naturally tend to respond with shock and disbelief. Frequently they cannot allow themselves to believe what they have been told—it is too dreadful and too final. Parents often state openly, "We do not want to believe it." The future is too awful. The prospects are unbearable. Family members will say quite directly, "We are not going to accept it. We cannot accept it."

Many parents will continue to deny that their child is fatally ill as long as they possibly can. They may take the ill child from clinic to clinic, from doctor to doctor, from specialist to quack in the hope that someone, anyone, can give them a happier diagnosis, a more hopeful future. Some parents just cannot accept the possibility that their child might die—both for the child's sake and for their own (Stehbens, 1974). If this is the first child in the family to die, it may be the parents' only child. If the youngster is afflicted with a hereditary illness, he may be the only child the parents will ever have, and when they lose him, they know they will have no further children. Parents may try to prevent the child's symptoms from becoming too obvious. The youngster's weakness may be rationalized as a winter cold, even though the parents have been told he has a malignancy. Leukemic bruises may be explained away on the basis of a vitamin lack. Obvious weight loss may be outwardly dismissed as being due to, "he is off his food."

The family doctor should not totally stand in the way of the parents' search for a more favorable diagnosis. Because the child is truly their responsibility, the father and the mother must always feel sure that they have done their very best for the youngster. They have to know that they have not failed to obtain for their child the most accurate diagnosis or the best treatment. Also, the process of adaptation and acceptance of a fatal diagnosis often takes time. To help the parents deal with their understandable shock and realistic dismay and to assist them in coping with the diagnosis, the physician may even suggest that they seek a second or third medical opinion to confirm the diagnosis. In this fashion, the doctor shows he understands their feeling and their wish that this diagnosis should be proven wrong. By his support, the physican helps the family members to begin to deal with their reaction. If he helps them get the best diagnosis, he remains the ally of the family and can then continue to be a source of strength and support as the youngster dies. When he suggests that the family seek only one or two confirmatory opinions, the doctor is at the same time setting limits and controls for the family anxiety. In this very practical way, he is implying that the family must eventually adapt so that the dying child can be given the greatest help for the final task.

As parents and family members begin to face the reality that the child is dying, they must accept the loss of a relationship that has been extremely meaningful. In most families, a child has a warm and positive relationship; his death will mean the loss of happiness and pleasure. In some unfortunate and less happy families, children are seen only as a burden or as a cause of pain and anguish; the loss of such a child may be anticipated with relief and even pleasure. Regardless of whether a child has been the source of joy or pain in the family, his death will in some way mean a difference and a change in the family. Any loss means that those left behind have to go through a process of mourning in one way or another. They have to adapt to a changed family. If the dying child made his family happy and has brought pleasure to his parents, his brothers and his sisters, the family members face the fact that they will no longer see his smile or hear his voice. His laugh, his teasing, will be absent from the dinner table. His room will be strangely tidy and quiet. The family phone will be silent, no more friends will be calling, but it will be the silence of death. Where the child has brought conflict and anger to the family, his death will bring a quietness to the turmoil. No longer will the parents have to tolerate the nagging and the bickering, but they will have to readjust to the peace, and they will have to find something else to do. The neighbors may be friendlier when the delinquent child is dead, but the family will have to adapt to this change in neighborhood attitude. If the dying child has had any impact on the family at all, happy or unhappy, productive or disruptive, this family will have to mourn his dying and his death.

As they face the fact that the child is dying, the family members cope in their own way. Each person who knows the child is dying responds to this information in the way he handles other life stresses and in a fashion compatible with his own character pattern, life-style and level of maturity. Some families, individually or as a family unit, show differing stages in their adaptation to the child's fatal illness (Kubler-Ross, 1969; Lieberman, 1978). There are no fixed stages and no universal patterns of coping with the death of a child or an adult (Bugen, 1977; Hudson, 1978).

People in the community and professionals on the treatment team must be alert to the individual way the family adapts to this very difficult situation. Parents may feel physically tired and have less strength for day-to-day activities. The mother may find that she has neither the inclination nor the strength to carry out her usual household chores; home is likely to become less tidy, the meals more haphazard, and mother may feel that she is failing the family. The father may notice that he is not quite as good at his work, and he makes more errors. The teachers may notice that the other children in the family are listless and irritable. Even though they are sad, sorrowing family members usually do not feel any marked loss of self-esteem. As they think and feel about this child who is about to leave them in death, their deeper feelings of warmth and love for the child and for each other help them feel an even deeper sense of self-worth. When family members come to realize how deeply they can care and are capable of caring, they often recognize how much they do give and how much they have given. As they mourn the child who is leaving them, the mourning family members may achieve a stronger sense of self-value.

During this normal adaptation to the fact that the child is dying, the mourning family members are liable to feel anger and irritation at this loss that they are experiencing. They are giving up a relationship that has been meaningful to them, meaningfully positive or meaningfully negative. With good reason, they resent the fact that they are being made to change or suffer in this way. The child's illness and death is causing them pain. Mourning family members may become worried and even guilty because they sense that they feel angry at the child who is dying. Logically they understand that the dying child does not want to die, but they find that they are increasingly irritable towards him. Since, in most instances, they do care deeply for the dying child, family members do not vent their grieving anger on the child who is going to leave them in death, but as part of normal mourning, the mourners need some way to express and work out this normal mourning anger. Frequently the parents find themselves more irritable towards each other. Brothers and sisters can be quite nasty to one another. In some families, bitter accusations are made—sometimes accusations that the child's death has been caused or allowed by negligence within the family. Illogical, resentful statements can be made, violent threats can be expressed, and all because these family members care deeply, grieve greatly and are angry because the dying child is leaving them. Families may need help so that they do not unload their mourning anger on each other in this unproductive way. This rage merely adds to the emotional burden of the family and of the dying child.

Quite often sorrowing relatives turn their mourning anger inward on themselves. The grieving father blames himself for not being present when his child dashed across the road; he is attacking himself, and he is likely to become depressed. The sorrowing mother feels that she has failed her child; if only she had fed him better, clothed him more warmly, then perhaps he could have resisted the leukemia. She vents her mourning anger on herself, and she is apt to become profoundly depressed. Brothers and sisters may feel guilty because they were not better protectors, and they feel bad. They may remember with shame the times that they were rough with this youngster who is now dying. The anguish of the family is often recognized very clearly by the dying child who may then become concerned because these people he loves are suffering. Frequently the dying youngster becomes the comforter to the other family members; the struggles of the mourning family may become the burden of the dying child. Other relatives and members of the treatment team need to be aware of the family mourning process and should help the grieving relatives and friends channel their mourning anger in a productive fashion.

If the child is dying with a hereditary illness, the guilt of one parent or the other is often very high. When it is clear where the genetic linkage lies, the parent responsible is liable to become the major focus of the family mourning anger, spoken and unspoken.

Very often the treatment team members find that the family mourning anger is unloaded on them. The physician, who is usually recognized by the family as being the head of the treatment team, appears strong and assured to the mourners. The doctor can be seen also as a suitable target for the grief anger of the family, as they may say to themselves, "He can take it." However, any member of the treating staff may become the focus for the family anger that is part of normal mourning. Sensitive treatment team members are often greatly upset when they feel that not only are their efforts on behalf of the dying child apparently unappreciated by the family, but also they are being abused and accused by these relatives. The caring team must understand that this family anger may be merely an outward expression of the anger inherent in any normal process of mourning.

While the treatment staff should not take this resentment as being personally caused, they will find that this anger complicates the treatment process at times. The family doctor is liable to be more annoyed when he is called out at three in the morning because the dying child has a twinge of pain. This seemingly unnecessary call may be just one manifestation of the family mourning resentment. "If we are kept awake, so can he." The sensitive and efficient nurse may find herself suddenly abused by family members because she is several minutes late in changing the child's dressing. This anger may appear to be totally unreasonable to the nurse until she remembers how angry the family must be at this child's dying. Then she can understand that the family members are directing some of their mourning anger on her. Many of the normal misfortunes or mishaps that occur in the treatment of a dying child may precipitate a sudden outburst of family rage—the pain that lasts too long, the bleeding that recurs, the vomiting that is not totally controlled. The caring staff must be very careful that they do not respond to any seemingly excessive or illogical family anger in an irrational fashion themselves. They should not react to an attack with a counterattack lest they add an even greater load of guilt and resentment on the shoulders of the suffering relatives. At the same time, professionals who are responsible for the care of the child do not need to tolerate unrealistic and unproductive anger. In a quiet moment, it is often helpful to empathize with the sadness or the anger of the sorrowing family. "Yes, it is very trying for you right now. You must feel very angry about what is happening."

The family who grieve about the fact that their child is fatally ill will need help to channel their mourning anger in a productive fashion. It is much more useful to the child and to the family if the parents express their mourning anger by battling the disease rather than by abusing the doctors—by joining cancer prevention societies, by campaigning for better cancer research, by championing earlier cancer detection. Mourning family members can lead crusades for leukemia investigation and can use their resentment constructively in fighting this dread disease. The programs for muscular dystrophy research, for cystic fibrosis camps and for many other worthwhile volunteer projects can be sponsored and coordinated by friends and relatives of children who are dying or who have died from these illnesses (Craig, 1977). The anger of the mourning process can be directed so that it leads to prevention and cure for others (Limerick, 1978).

As part of any mourning process, parents and members of the dying child's family should reinvest emotionally. They must begin to change their goals and their plans. After they have been told the diagnosis, the parents and the family will start to look on the dying child as a different person. He can never be the same again. He is now unique and special. In some families, the parents and the relatives find a certain gratification in dealing with a child who is fatally ill. Now again they can nurse, they can baby, and they can protect this child. The family may almost like having an invalid in their midst and in some ways may even encourage the child's invalidism. Sometimes it is apparent that the relatives are really expressing their mourning anger towards the child by keeping him overprotected, whether he likes it or not. This is socially a very acceptable way of expressing rage at the dying child who is causing everyone this pain.

Everyone in a family tends to identify with every other person in that family in some fashion. Parents see themselves in their children, and the children can recognize their own traits in their parents and in each other. When parents watch their child dying, they can sense in him a shadow of their own approaching death. Brothers and sisters may look at the child who is dying and feel an affinity that makes them very anxious. When a family member has a fatal illness, his dying may remind those around him much too much of their own vulnerability. If their identification with the dying child is very strong, the family members may have to keep away from the child because the youngster makes them think too strongly about the possibility of their own death. If a loving father has believed that his child has many of his characteristics, he may become quite anxious when this son begins to die in front of him; he can almost see himself dying. If a mother has based many of her own hopes and goals on her daughter's prospects, she is likely to find it difficult to visit this daughter when she is dying; the mother can sense that her own future is going into the grave also. When a child has died, it is not often very helpful when the nurse or the physician says to the grieving family, "He is much better off now where he is." No parent, no brother, no sister and no family member likes to be told that a part of himself or herself is better dead (Keeler, 1954; Greene and Miller, 1958).

Parents often find it difficult to deal with the fatal illness and death of a newborn child. Nurses, doctors and family members are liable to see this very young child as an inanimate object, as a "thing." The mother and the father have lived with this child for nine months during the pregnancy, and the mother especially has felt the child's movements and responded to its developing personality, imagined or real.

The single parent can be especially burdened with the task of mourning the child that is dying. This parent, mother or father, may have fewer relatives or friends to turn to for support or solace. The blame and the guilt for the child's illness or accident is more likely to land on the single parent. The single parent may have other unavoidable continuing responsibilities that make it difficult to see the child as often as the child needs and the parent wishes. The treating staff should be alert to the special needs of the child and the relatives.

Because parents identify strongly with their children, they are apt to be deeply upset by the appearance of the dying child (Richmond and Waisman, 1955; Martin, Lawrie, and Wilkinson, 1968). They have loved their child when he was well, so they are likely to be distressed when he becomes disfigured before their eyes. They are also prone to be concerned because they can see themselves in the child who is dying there in front of their eyes. Because they are so bothered by the child's appearance, grieving relatives may be unable to visit the dying youngster disfigured by burns, tumors or leukemic bruises and bleeding. Changes in the child's appearance due to treatment procedures or medications are prone to make the family very uneasy. If the dying child develops a toxic reaction to a drug, suffers loss of hair or develops a skin rash, the grieving parents are likely to become more anxious and less able to support the treatment. When the dying child is no longer pretty or cute and does not even look like a child, the relatives may look for an excuse to stay away.

Family members should be encouraged to continue visiting the dying child, both for the child's sake and for their own emotional adaptation. If the parents and relatives did stay away from the child, not only would they have to deal with their own guilt at this rejection, but they would also have to face their own fantasies about the child's appearance. These fantasies are liable to be even more nightmarish than any reality. The treating staff should monitor how the child is being visited and must take care that parents and family members do not use the visiting regulations as an excuse to avoid the youngster who is dying. Parents who feel anxious may prompt members of the treatment team into saying something that would justify their staying away. "He gets tired very easily, doesn't he?" "He does not understand what is going on." "She is busy with the other patients." If just one of the treating staff agrees, the parents may use this as a rationalization for not coming to see the dying child. Unless the parents and the close family members are obviously and deeply disturbed by the very stressful situation, they should be expected to continue visiting and not to desert the child in his time of maximum need. However, it is important that the nurse or the doctor recognize the stress the family is facing and work with them to lower their tension. Often it helps the mother a great deal to tell someone, anyone, how hard it is for her to watch her beautiful daughter slip away. Frequently, a guilty father feels much better when he shares with a sympathetic ear his feelings of fear when he sees his child fading from day to day.

Every parent feels a certain responsibility for his own children, no matter how old these children may be or how distant the relationship might have become. No matter how much a mother may dislike her own child, she usually feels some sense of duty towards him. No matter how angry or rejecting a father may have become towards his sons and daughters, he can never totally avoid having some personal commitment towards these children. Thus, when a child begins to die, the most natural response of the parents is to feel that, in some way, they have failed their basic parental responsibility. The dying child already tends to blame his parents and his family for what is happening to him, and he senses the way that his relatives blame themselves. As he deals with his own dying and faces his own anger at what is happening to him, the dying child may sometimes abuse and rage at his parents and family, and the family members may too readily accept the blame.

Frequently, family members blame themselves because they did not understand that the youngster was ill or they were not aware of his sufferings. Before the child was diagnosed, he may have been tired and irritable due to a leukemic process, and the parents may have been angry with him because of his behavior. When the disease is recognized, the parents are liable to feel guilty because of what they did. If nausea, vomiting or bedwetting were early symptoms of a brain tumor, the mother quite naturally may have felt this behavior was due to childishness or poor self-control. When she learns that the child is fatally ill, she is likely to become upset when she remembers what she said. If the little boy has stumbled because of the weakness of developing muscular dystrophy, his brothers and sisters may have teased him in their play. When they learn of his diagnosis, they are apt to feel guilty because of what they thought. Teachers may reprimand a school child for seeming laziness or stupidity only to learn, with much guilt, that these were the early symptoms of this youngster's fatal illness.

When the diagnosis of a fatal illness is made, the child's parents

The Dying Child

are likely to feel very helpless. Often they do not fully understand the meaning of the diagnosis. They certainly cannot direct the evaluation and treatment procedures. They are forced to allow the physician to make the decisions for their child, and when the youngster is hospitalized, the doctor takes over even more of the parents' authority. The treating staff increasingly makes the decisions that the parents used to make. Though the family delegates its responsibility to the caring personnel in order to benefit the child, they certainly will have mixed feelings at this change of authority. The parents and the family tend to see themselves relegated to being mere visitors with their own child. The caring staff have now become parents to the parents as well as to the ill youngster. The sick child senses this change and realizes that his parents are relatively powerless in this new situation. The parents have become merely older siblings in the family unit that they once directed. Because the parents are more helpless, the dying child can more easily vent his anger and bitterness on them. "You do not care. You left me here in hospital." The youngster may even taunt them with their ineffectiveness. "You can't do anything."

The parents, who are already grieving over the approaching death of their child, will struggle with the fact that they are no longer in control of their child's destiny and that they find themselves attacked by this dying child for whom they care and for whom they are mourning. In such a situation, the parents and family members will need a great deal of team support and understanding. The doctor and other treatment personnel should insist that the parents continue to be involved in all decisions regarding the child. They must continue as parents, as the most important decision makers, in collaboration with the clinical team. It should be recognized that the final decision, even a decision for or against treatment, always rests with the parents. At the same time, the parents may need protection from the child's resentment. The treatment team should not allow the dying child to abuse any member of his family, emotionally or physically. At all times, the clinical team must be aware that they are treating not only the dying child but also the mourning family, the family that will live on after the child is gone.

When the child is hospitalized, both he and his parents have to face their anxieties over this separation (Bierman, 1956). The anxious parents may be very loath to let the child leave home because they feel, with some reality, that he may never again return to them. They worry that, once they let him out of their control, they will lose him forever, and this indeed is inevitably so. The fatally ill child, once hospitalized, never comes back the same child. The child will sense his parents' fears and may be even more reluctant and more fearful to enter the hospital. When the youngster goes to the hospital, he very quickly recognizes that he has passed into a realm where his parents do not have control. At the same time, even though they are anxious and fearful about hospitalization, the parents may be eager to see the child placed in the hospital. In face of their fears, they may hope for a miracle cure. Somehow, in that big and overwhelming hospital, their child must be made healthy.

When parents are told that their youngster has a fatal illness, they often feel that they have suddenly been burdened with an overwhelming responsibility. Once this child leaves home and becomes a hospital responsibility, he ceases to be an immediate problem to the parents, so this heavy burden is taken from their shoulders. They may be very hesitant about letting the child leave, but they may also be very relieved to see him go. If he bleeds, there is someone in the hospital to care for him. If he has a convulsion, the hospital personnel know what to do. If he loses weight, the nurses have been trained to nourish him. Because the parents have so many fears and such hopes, the doctor may become invested with magical or even supernatural powers in the eyes of the family. Since they fear so much, they may hope for and expect so much.

Because the doctor and the treating staff do not perform this miracle, the family sometimes become resentful and angry. They have been able to deny the impact of the child's disease by hoping that the doctor would be able to perform a miracle, but when the fallible physician does not bring a miraculous cure, the family denial cannot be maintained. Their anger and anxiety are liable to be expressed in resentment towards the physician or the nurses who did not perform in the way the family had so unrealistically hoped.

In the hospital, the day-to-day problems of the child's illness are handled by the professional staff. Each symptom is dealt with by the treating personnel according to the hospital routine. The family of the child comes to depend more and more on the regulations and the structure of the hospital. When everything is planned and programmed in this fashion, the family can relax and allow themselves to fit into the hospital routines. When the child is about to be allowed home because he has had a symptomatic remission or is improved, the members of his family are likely then to become more anxious. They now fear that they will be unable to cope with this child. What should they do if he suddenly becomes ill again? They think of him as fragile or easily damaged and hesitate to control or discipline him. The family now sees the child as a very different person from the youngster who left home.

The child's mother bears the greatest burden of these family fears and responsibilities when the fatally ill child returns home. She may become so protective of the child that she keeps the child isolated and away from healthy social contacts. Because they do not know quite how to handle the child who is so ill, the other family members tend to move out of the home during his visit; the children stay at school, the father remains late at work, and the mother is left alone now to deal with this child who has been given back to her by the hospital. When he returns home, the fatally ill youngster may have nothing to do. His friends and siblings are at school. The sick youngster soon learns he can demand and his family will do what he wants. Merely by his presence, he can be the center of attention. In this situation, the family and especially the mother needs the constant support of the hospital team. If the mother knows that she can call the treatment personnel for a consultation at any time, she can be more relaxed in dealing with the child. If she is certain that the youngster can be immediately rehospitalized in an emergency, she and other family members can deal much more realistically with the youngster on a day-to-day basis (Tisza, 1962; Friedman, Chodoff, Mason and Hamburg, 1963).

When the sick child is sent home from the hospital, some parents take this as a sign that the youngster has been cured. Why else would the doctors send the child home? Because of their fears, the parents are apt to use the child's discharge from hospital to reinforce their hopes. On the other hand, other parents are prone to see their child's discharge from hospital as an indication that the doctors and nurses feel that nothing can be done for the youngster. Hospital discharge is liable to make these parents feel more hopeless and despairing. Prior to any discharge from hospital, the treating staff must talk with the parents and the family members in detail about the child's clinical situation and the purpose of a home visit or a decision to discharge the child from hospital. The clinicians must help the family not to have unrealistic hopes or irrational fears.

When the fatally ill child is at home, he should live as much as possible as part of his family, but the hospital team should be available at all times to the family members for counseling and to answer their questions. The presence of the sick child at home is liable to cause a great deal of tension and turmoil. His brothers and sisters are likely to see him as a "special child" who is receiving special family attention. At times they may resent this preferential treatment and then feel guilty at their resentment. Siblings may feel angry at the child who is dying because he takes up so much of the parents' time and makes the family so sad. Brothers and sisters may not outwardly show their anger at the sick youngster but rather may express their irritation at each other. This family anxiety and anger only adds to the emotional burdens of the parents, who have to manage the dying child at home. The fatally ill youngster sometimes capitalizes on his special status. If he does not get his own way, the sick child may taunt his parents with the fact that he is dying, and how can they treat him this way? Sometimes the sick youngster allows his illness to become more apparent as one way to manipulate his family and the people around him.

If the fatally ill youngster continues to go to school, and this should always be encouraged whenever the child is physically capable, teachers also will need help to make this a productive experience for the youngster (Bauer, 1976). Too often the fatally ill child at school is treated like a pathological specimen. Principals, teachers and teachers' aides look on the ill youngster as "the boy with cancer" or "the girl with leukemia" rather than as Johnny or Mary whom they have known for so many years. They respond more to the sickness than to the child who is ill.

Frequently, the child's continued outpatient treatment also puts a heavy burden on the family, and especially on the mother. If the youngster has to attend a treatment center, there is the strain of the travel to the clinics. The family routine is disturbed. Sometimes father has to take time away from work or mother has to stop working with added financial cost to the family. Too many hospital and clinic waiting rooms are lonely, foreboding and menacing to the parents and children who attend (Hoffman, 1971). The announcements about the latest meeting of the leukemia society or the posters inviting contributions for cancer research emphasize illness and death. In the waiting room sit other children and families who know that their time also is short. Few waiting rooms and clinics emphasize the joys of living and the need to live life to the fullest, even though the span may be short or uncertain.

When a child is dying of a chronic illness, the course of his disease is likely to be long, variable and unpredictable (Bozeman, Orbach, and Sutherland, 1955). Sometimes, unexpectedly and without explanation, he may get worse or better. This fluctuation in the illness course often makes life very difficult for other members of the family. Relatives find that they are trying constantly to adjust to a changing reality. When a youngster seems to be getting sicker, family members may resign themselves to the child's impending death only to find that the child unexpectedly begins to get well again. They then begin to adapt to this improvement and to the hope that the youngster may live, but when they have adjusted to this change, they may find again that unpredictably the child has become ill once more. When the child's sickness is prolonged and shows remissions and exacerbations, his family find it very difficult to plan ahead. They cannot control his illness, they cannot be sure what next week or next month will bring, and they are unable to get the child out of their minds. Eventually, family members are likely to become very frustrated. They realize with resentment that their lives are being controlled by the illness of this one sick child. Almost in spite of themselves, they are liable to become angry, and this anger can be expressed toward the child or toward members of the treatment team. Caring relatives sometimes find themselves wishing that the child would die—often with great guilt and anxiety—so that everything could become settled and predictable. This thought, however fleeting, is likely to make family members very ashamed, but the dying child begins to sense that his continued existence is becoming more of a burden on his family. He finds that his improvement is welcomed less. The youngster in this unfortunate situation is liable to become even more lonely and depressed when he realizes his parents are becoming tired of him.

The family has no option but to live through this very trying situation in as productive a fashion as possible, but it is often very helpful if members of the treatment team can talk openly with the family about the difficulties of dealing with changing illness.

The Living Dead

As part of the normal process of mourning, family members must withdraw their emotional investment in the child who is dying and reinvest their energy in other people and other things that will continue. This withdrawal of emotional ties is usually a gradual process, which goes on during the course of the child's illness and is finalized after he is dead. Sometimes this farewell and reinvesting process does not occur in a healthy or timely fashion.

When the child's parents are unable to face the fact that their child is dying, they make it impossible for themselves to work through the necessary anticipatory mourning before the child does die. When the youngster actually dies, parents can no longer deny this unpleasant and painful reality and then show a sudden, profound mourning reaction. All at once, they have to face their inescapable feelings of sadness and anger and must adapt to an abrupt loss.

If the fatally ill child takes a long time to die, the parents and the family members may have worked through most of the mourning process even before he dies. While he is still alive, the family may have said good-bye to the child and then have a very few meaningful emotional ties left with him. Their visits then become perfunctory and merely a family duty. Their conversation and their play with the dying child are likely to be merely a way of passing the time rather than an important interaction. The child's toys, clothing and other belongings may be given away before the youngster is actually dead. The funeral is already arranged. In such situations, the youngster may be emotionally dead as far as the family is concerned while he is still physically alive; he is "the living dead" (Rosner, 1962; Green and Solnit, 1964; Kalish, 1966b).

This syndrome of the living dead can occur even when the child dies relatively quickly. In some families, the parents and relatives withdraw their emotional investment in the dying child very quickly and reinvest abruptly. When they are told that the child has a fatal illness, they begin to respond right away as if he were dead. Even though the child may continue to live for quite some time, he is surrounded by family members who are interested in other things and other people. The parents may adopt another child (Nolfi, 1967). The mother may become pregnant with another infant. The father may develop other long-range projects.

When family members see other families with youngsters who are dying, sometimes they do their mourning by proxy (Hoffman, 1971). Parents who attend a leukemia clinic with their child may go through much of their mourning as they watch the other children in the clinic die. The parents who take their child to regular renal dialysis see the other youngsters being dialyzed and will watch their progress or deterioration. In these circumstances, sometimes parents work through much of their mourning with the other children who die before their youngster.

Where the child is chronically ill, the youngster and his parents are subject to repeated emotional assaults by the ongoing diagnostic and treatment process (Drotar and Ganofsky, 1977). The therapeutic management wears everybody down—the child, the family and the treatment team. Even though the youngster remains alive, eventually the relatives become exhausted, and then it is easier to say farewell. When family members have mourned him too early and too completely, the fatally ill child will find himself isolated and alone. He has been mourned and laid to rest even before he is dead.

Sometimes this syndrome of living death occurs through mutual agreement between the dying child and his grieving family. Most children care deeply for their parents and their relatives and do not wish to cause them pain. The family members do not want to hurt the child in any way. When the youngster is dying, the child and his family inevitably realize that the child's dying distresses everyone. Because they do care very deeply for each other, the child and his family sometimes allow and even encourage each other to drift apart emotionally. Then it is easier on everyone. The fatally ill youngster begins to make fewer and fewer emotional demands on his parents, and they react by becoming less concerned and less available. This mutual denial process allows the parents to insulate themselves more completely from the pain of the child's dying and permits the child to isolate himself from the pain of his family's misery. Most youngsters are very solicitous of their family and relatives and will try to keep those they love from feeling pain, even the pain of mourning their own death (Adsett, 1968). As the dying child gets nearer to death, he may make this final effort to protect his family by allowing them to withdraw from him emotionally.

The syndrome of the living dead occurs when the grieving family withdraws emotional investment too soon from the sick child, when the fatally ill youngster and his family mutually agree to pull back from each other or when the child himself protects his family by withdrawing from them. While the treatment team must be aware of the factors that cause this premature mourning or early separation, it should not allow the early farewells to become too absolute or too fixed. This child's family must continue to be involved in all aspects of the total treatment if the therapeutic procedures are to be maximally efficient. At the same time, the family and the dying child should continue relating to each other, even in a minimal fashion, so that the separation inherent in death is worked through in an integrated, adaptive fashion that gives the child peace and allows continued family emotional growth. In this era when many fatally ill children live for years, treatment team members will deal frequently with youngsters who have outlived the family mourning and who merely wait for death.

The Lazarus Syndrome

And he that was dead came forth.
John 11:44

The Lazarus syndrome is relatively rare in clinical practice but may cause management problems when it does occur. Typically there is a certain sequence of events leading to this syndrome. First, the child is diagnosed correctly as having a disease that is usually fatal or becomes so severely ill that death appears inevitable. The parents and family members recognize the reality of the child's situation or meaning of the diagnosis. Death increasingly gets nearer, and everyone mourns the child appropriately. Then, unexpectedly, the youngster recovers or enters into an extended remission. The drug or the radiotherapeutic procedure may have destroyed the neoplastic process. The youngster recovers from prolonged coma. The child miraculously survives injuries that are usually fatal. In this situation, the family and the child may then be faced with a difficult emotional readjustment (Green and Solnit, 1964).

If the child has been mourned realistically and appropriately, he will then find that his family has left him emotionally. As part of the mourning process, the family is likely to have adjusted to a future without the child. They have adapted to the fact that they were helpless in dealing with their child's situation (Benjamin, 1978). In some of these families, it is very difficult for the recovered child to become reintegrated again as a family member. The youngster who recovers from an illness that is usually fatal is likely to return to his family as if he were in some way a new family member—as if he were just born or reborn. The youngster who recovers from a usually fatal illness does not come back to the family as the same child with the same position in his family. He returns into a family as if he has been dead and has come back to life because he has been mourned, mourned reasonably and mourned in a healthy fashion. As part of this mourning process, he and his family actually did say farewell to each other. If he now recovers from what typically is a fatal illness, he has to move back into his family as a new member. His parents, his brothers and sisters and his close relatives have the difficult emotional task of adapting to a different child, a child who was ill, died, but recovered.

The treatment team and the family will have to deal with this unexpected situation realistically. The dying child can never go through his illness and recover and still be seen as the same child that he was before. When Lazarus returns from the grave, he comes back not as a beloved brother but as a stranger from a strange land; a relative who has to become known again and loved once more.

When the child is dying, his parents and his family are reinvesting emotionally as part of the process of normal mourning. The parents find at the same time, however, that they are still expected to continue a heavy financial investment in this child (Nolfi, 1967). When the child is fatally ill, the family are obliged to devote their material resources to a project that has no future. As the sorrowing family begin to plan for a time when the dying child will have gone, they are still expected to spend an increasing percentage of the family resources, financial and emotional, on this child. Eventually the family is likely to resent the continued or increasing financial and emotional burden. Hospital administrative personnel are likely to find that parents of fatally ill children become more bitter and less cooperative about the hospital bills. When the child is dead and gone, the parents are apt to react angrily and sometimes explosively when they find themselves still expected to expend family resources on paying hospital and doctor bills. In many ways the family is likely to feel that the investment is completed and the chapter is finished when the child is dead. The continued financial involvement after the youngster has been completely mourned seems to have little purpose. The parents then have to deal with this persistent obligation at a time when they are increasingly transferring their emotional energies to other, more lasting and more productive interests.

As the child learns very early that there is an acceptable social way of dying, so parents and family members find that there is a socially correct way of dealing with their child's approaching death (Thomas, 1972). Though mourning relatives in Western countries no longer have mourning clothes (Eissler, 1955), they are still expected to conform to certain social patterns of behavior. In most industrialized nations, sorrowing parents are expected to be depressed and withdrawn. The family members may feel lonely and alone in their sadness, but they dare not try too obviously to seek relief from their grief. If mourning parents go to a movie or a dance while their child is dying in an effort to lessen their sorrow temporarily, they are liable to be socially labeled as bad, unfeeling parents. If the parents of a fatally ill child dare laugh or joke too freely, they are apt to be ostracized socially because society expects them to be downcast and solemn.

The mother of the dying child may want to wear an attractive, colorful dress to boost her flagging spirits, but she is liable to find herself condemned for being unfeeling or frivolous if she wears such clothes. The father of the dying child might find it a great help to work off his tension in a football game or in playing golf, but he may find that his athletic activity is viewed as callous self-indulgence by many members of his social group. He is not expected to enjoy himself. The brother of the fatally ill child may find that his teacher or his peers are uncomfortable if he laughs too often. The sister of the dying child is likely to be reprimanded if she has the audacity to go to the school dance. How can she dance when her brother is dying? How can he joke when his sister is fatally ill? When the child is dying over a period of months or years, the social isolation imposed on the members of his family will make their emotional burden more difficult to tolerate. Family members who face this situation together can support one another, but the unmarried mother or the single parent can be especially lonely if her child is dying (Craig, 1977).

Grieving family members are likely to find that they have become more socially distanced when their child is dying and for a period after the child's death. They are isolated more from their community at a time when they need their social contacts most. They will find that they carry the stigma of the child's illness with them (Gyulay, 1978). As the dying are avoided in our society, so are the companions and the relatives of death (Raphael, 1977). This family isolation is likely to be greater when the dying child has a physical illness that is especially threatening in his culture. Cancer in industrialized nations is especially threatening, so relatives of the child dying of cancer may find themselves more isolated. The effects of leukemia have been well publicized, so parents of the child dying with leukemia may find that other parents tend to avoid them. Muscular dystrophy research has been emphasized in many countries, and parents of muscular dystrophy children will find themselves more understood but also more isolated. Each culture has plagues that are feared and that each society and each community tends to shun.

The relatives of the dying child must understand that their

close relationship to death makes other people tense and anxious. As mourners, they have a responsibility to the child who is dying, to themselves and to their own family, but they also have a role to play in their community The treating team must appreciate how each level of responsibility adds another burden to the load that the bereaved family members must bear.

Chapter Six

THE TREATING PERSONNEL

Everyone who comes into contact with the dying child should be considered an important member of the treatment team. When the cleaning lady tidies the child's bedside table, the gentle way she squeezes his hand may help him sleep more securely than all the sedatives he receives that day. The maintenance man who jokes with the little dying girl while he repairs the electric light fixture may give the youngster enough strength to tolerate another transfusion or medication dose. The silent tear of the young nurse, when the ward team does rounds, may reveal the truth to the dying child in spite of the overconfident smile of the physician team leader. In working effectively with the child who is nearing death, it is necessary to coordinate the activities of all the people who relate in any fashion to the child—the maintenance men, kitchen helpers, priests, school teachers, cleaning ladies, nurses, parents, physicians, aides, gardeners and even the ladies who sell the candy and the comics; all must work together to help each other and to help this child die as comfortably as possible for everyone.

Most human beings provide treatment for others because of the rewards they receive in return. When it comes to dealing with the dying child, the recompense for increasingly difficult work may be more and more uncertain, meager and unsatisfying. Treating personnel tend to enjoy giving care because their patients get better; the caring people can feel useful, good and powerful. Most clinicians need to feel efficient (Weisskopf and Binder, 1976). When a patient gets well, the treating staff can feel that they have conquered disease. They are gratified because they have assisted another human being. These are very pleasant feelings that most people enjoy. When a youngster is dying, the caring staff sometimes think that the rewards of therapeutic success are absent. Periodically the treatment team members lose hope. As the youngster's illness progresses, the clinicians are liable to feel increasingly impotent. Many doctors, nurses and aides find themselves avoiding any patient who makes them feel helpless, worthless or despairing in this way. If the fatally ill patient is being seen in psychotherapy, the psychotherapist may stop the psychotherapy treatment because the patient has started to die.

When "the case" has become obviously hopeless, the doctor may begin to give only minimal treatment and cursory attention. The nurse is more likely to spend time with other, more interesting patients because she does not wish to waste her time unnecessarily with someone who is bound to be a treatment failure. People look with pity on the dying child and then pass on, but often they pass because they would be too uncomfortable at their own helplessness if they stayed. They go on to other patients because it is more comfortable to avoid awkward situations and feelings.

Traditionally, certain members of the treatment team are expected to be stronger and more steadfast. The physician, especially, is looked to for guidance, since he is usually considered to be the leader of the therapeutic team. As team leader, he has the responsibility of telling the parents about the diagnosis and the prognosis. If he really wants to be the team leader, the doctor cannot avoid this responsibility to the child and family. When he comes to share the facts about the youngster's illness and treatment with the child's family, he should tell both parents at the same time. As the parents learn about the child's illness together, they can support each other (Howell, 1966). They can ask questions together or in turn and begin to comfort each other as they learn the answers. The doctor has not fulfilled his duty merely by telling the parents the diagnosis and the prognosis for the child's illness. As leader of the treatment team, responsible for the whole family, he should make himself available for the questions that inevitably will arise during the course of the child's illness. Whenever he talks with the parents, the doctor should recognize that he has taken on himself the responsibility of choosing the information that the parents are to know, and he should be very clear in his own mind why he shares certain information and why he avoids other facts (Garfield, 1978).

While the physician, nurses, aides and other members of the treatment team need to be able to identify with the feelings and the struggles of their young dying patient, this sympathy and understanding should not undermine their main treatment purpose. They must give the child the treatment he needs as efficiently as possible. The doctor always has to be a source of strength to the family and to the other members of the treatment team. If he identifies so intensely with the dying child and his family that he allows himself to cry or to appear confused or overwhelmed in front of the family members, he will have failed his patient and the family in this time of great need. The physician and the other members of the treatment team should allow themselves to have deep feelings for the patient, but they must show by their example how these feelings can be controlled and channeled. The relatives of the dying child are liable to become understandably angry towards a staff member, doctor or nurse, who is overcome by his sadness, his anger or his powerlessness, even though the family can appreciate the reason for these feelings. The doctor who allows his feelings about the dying child to cause him so much anguish that he becomes silent in his discussions with the parents leaves these stricken family members without the support they need. A prolonged, awkward silence when the clinicians are telling the parents or family members about the youngster's situation will usually lead to increased tension and fear because the family can feel, with some justification, that no one is in control of the situation. In talking with the parents and relatives, some silences should be tolerated and supported, but these are the silences that occur when meaningful emotions are being felt and shown, when the family members need time for quiet, profound sadness. The silences that should be allowed are not empty silences but are periods of intense and necessary feeling. At such a time, the team member who is talking with the parents is still in control of the interview but is supporting the expression and the working through of appropriate feelings.

Sometimes the physician, the treatment leader, is so bothered by the fact that his patient is dying that he avoids the patient's family. He becomes busy in some other place during visiting hours. He has appointments elsewhere when the parents are on the hospital unit. In these circumstances, the nursing staff are liable to find themselves under increasing pressure from family members who reasonably want to know what is happening to the child. The child's relatives can guess the gravity of the youngster's situation from the appearance of the child and the attitude of the nurses, but the nurses may feel that they cannot be open and direct without the doctor's permission. Eventually in these circumstances, the nursing staff may be forced to tell the family what is happening to the child because the child's reality may be too obvious. By his withdrawal, however, the doctor may have forced the nursing staff to act in his place and to assume his responsibilities. Too often then, the doctor becomes angry with the nurses or aides who have told the child or the family members the facts of the situation, and the physician may complain that these other members of the treatment team have overstepped their professional responsibilities. In reality, much of the anger the doctor feels and shows may arise from his own guilt because he has failed the family and the team members and from his own feelings of powerlessness in face of the child's approaching death. The doctor and all other members of the treatment team, at every level of seniority, must accept the reality that eventually they are helpless when they deal with a patient who is about to die (Le Shan, 1961; Lourie, 1963; Howell, 1966). The treatment staff have to live with this helplessness. They must take care, however, lest they vent their discomfort and their anxiety on one another, on the patient's family or on the dying child himself.

Many treatment team members enjoy the warm relationships that arise amongst the staff of an active clinical unit and with the patients with whom they work so hard. When a patient is dying, sometimes the caring staff feel that all their hard work is not being really appreciated or effective. They begin to wonder whether somehow their efforts are being wasted. In an almost illogical fashion, they are likely then to blame the dying child for not appreciating or responding to their work. The feeling of the treating personnel may be almost, "How can he do this to us, after all we have done for him?" When these feelings develop, sensitive staff members may become very uncomfortable. They have to understand and cope with feelings, however, if they are going to continue to treat dying patients beneficially. They must recognize that their caring is likely to bring less appreciation if appreciation is measured in terms of patient improvement.

When members of the treating staff have a strong fellow feeling with a patient, it often makes it easier to work with this patient. The more readily the nurses can identify with a child or adolescent, the easier it is for these people to give warm nursing care. If the little girl reminds the sensitive nurse of her own sister, the nurse may be even more gentle; if the little girl is dying, the nurse also feels emotions that are harder to tolerate. If the physician can see himself in the muscular teenage patient, he may work harder to help the young man. If the teenager is dying, the doctor's empathy with the patient will undoubtedly raise awkward anxiety. When a patient is dying, treatment team members are likely to find that their empathy with the patient makes them increasingly uneasy. They become more uncomfortable because they can see themselves dying, as this patient is dying in front of their eyes. Where identification with the patient may have produced more enthusiastic treatment earlier, it is likely to lead to avoidance when it becomes apparent that the patient is dying. Then the young aides may be unable to pay attention to the dying teenager because she is so much like them in age and appearance. The doctor is more apt to hurry past the bed of the dying child because the little boy reminds him too keenly of his own son. The nurses start to talk over the patient rather than speak to him. They ask others how he feels rather than question him directly. Without realizing he has changed, the priest may rattle through his prayers because the young girl looks so much like his sister, and he feels heartsick and homesick.

Among the treatment team, there sometimes develops a covert agreement to isolate the dying patient (Glaser and Strauss, 1968). Very often, the child who is dying is moved to a side ward or to a more private room. Sometimes this transfer is justified on the basis that the youngster will have more privacy and better treatment, but in reality, the patient becomes more isolated, and the staff do not have to see him as much. Some dying patients are allowed unlimited visiting privileges even though they are exhausted by the constant stream of visitors. The staff can then be more comfortable if the dying child is surrounded and insulated away by a mob of relatives. The treatment team members find easier excuses to be busy with other patients. Treatment team members must always be aware of the heavy emotional burden that the dying patient places on the total treatment team, on the hospital unit and on the patient himself. If the dying child is isolated on the hospital treatment unit, this isolation will only occur at great psychological expense to the total unit treatment efficiency.

Because the professional team care for the dying patient, they are likely to develop strong and sometimes irrational feelings towards his family. The treatment members themselves are mourning the approaching death of this child patient, so they also have to handle their own sadness and grieving anger. Sometimes this anger is directed towards the family members. Grieving parents may be treated brusquely and coldly by the hospital staff, and the family find that the staff have become less helpful and less cooperative. In this situation, the treating personnel may be going through a normal process of mourning for this child who is dying, but they are expressing their mourning feelings unproductively by venting them on the parents. The dying child sometimes becomes furious and nasty towards his parents, and the youngster may find that the doctors and nurses not only tolerate this angry behavior but may almost encourage this abuse of the family. In this fashion, treatment team members permit the child to express the anger they feel because he is dying. Since they have this mourning bitterness, the hospital personnel may make life more difficult for the family of the patient than the staff realize.

Occasionally, treatment team members refuse to cooperate with the way the family handle their mourning. Some families handle their grieving by overcontrol, denial and intellectualization but find that their way of coping with the child's dying is considered by the treatment staff as indicating a lack of feeling. Some families express their mourning loudly and openly and may find then that the treatment team become angry with this behavior that the staff consider to be infantile or hysterical. Often the parents are expected to go through a series of stages in their responses to the child's death, and the treatment team become quite annoyed if the relatives do not mourn in the way the staff feel appropriate. This lack of team support for family grief may be one way the staff show their own mourning sadness and anger. Each member of the treatment team has to be aware of the feelings of other team members in coping with this difficult therapeutic situation. With understanding and firmness, the staff have to support and sometimes direct each other.

As part of their normal mourning, the caring staff should gradually reinvest emotionally as the dying child moves towards death. It is very easy, sometimes too easy, for the treatment team members to make this emotional reinvestment in the patient's family. If the caring professionals strongly identify with the child who is about to die, they can keep this emotional investment by developing strong bonds to the child's family. As the child approaches death, the caring personnel sometimes develop strong and occasionally nonprofessional relationships with family members of the dying patient. The treatment team members are likely to have many rationalizations as to why they have formed this special emotional bond with the patient's family. The nurses will protest that it is only kindness that leads them to spend long hours over coffee with the parents, since the family is visiting practically around the clock. The sympathetic physician may find many good reasons for driving the sorrowing parents home and for talking to them on the way in a warm and intimate fashion. These close emotional ties between relatives of the dying child and members of the treatment team may not always be helpful to the child or to his family. Eventually the mourning family must face the death of their child and must continue to grow with other projects and other people. The hospital personnel should take care that they do not bind the family to the hospital and thus to the child who will die. Some follow-up procedures have the effect of continuing to hold on emotionally to relatives who otherwise might have separated from the hospital where their child was ill and died. A follow-up study may hinder parents and family members from finally completing the natural growth process of mourning. Researchers should recognize that some of the angry responses they meet are due to the resentment of families because the research procedures do not allow the relatives to bring their mourning to final conclusion. The child should be allowed to die when he is dead.

Treating staff often enjoy their work because of the intellectual stimulation they meet. They like the challenge of the diagnosis, the gratification of treatment achievement and the pleasures of therapeutic success. When a child is dying, the professional staff have much less opportunity for this kind of gratification. Very often treating personnel try to keep the dying patient as an intellectual problem. The patient then becomes an exercise in life maintenance—and still that fascinating academic question. The youngster may be subjected to many treatment and diagnostic procedures until he has been exsanguinated for blood tests and exhausted by treatment procedures. The team that truly cares must beware that they do not reduce the dying child to a mere object or academic exercise. When the youngster is dying, the treatment team eventually has to face the reality that no number of tests or treatment procedures will alter the final outcome. When treating professionals see the patient primarily as an intellectual exercise, they also tend to forget the family and frequently do not give the relatives the support they need. Then, when the child dies, the staff suddenly appear to lose any remaining interest in the family, who are likely to feel abruptly abandoned.

In caring for the dying child, the team members will find that their roles are inextricably intertwined. The team is as strong as each member is strong, and no one professional or paraprofessional staff member has a monopoly of caring or strength. In helping their child live through this experience of death, the parents themselves are an essential part of the total, integrated treatment team. They and the other members of the family should interact with the treatment team in such a way that together they give the dying child the best treatment, the finest available care and the greatest comfort. Sometimes the child's parents can be helped to feel more useful and worthwhile if they have some meaningful hospital duties to perform with their child (Bierman, 1956). These responsibilities allow them to stay with the dying youngster and also to deal with their fears and anxieties in a more productive fashion.

On many clinical units, the clergyman is an important member of the treatment team and in such settings has a significant role with every child and every mourning family, no matter what the religious beliefs of that family are. Hinton (1963) suggested that adult dying patients had less anxiety in the face of death when they either had a firm religious belief or no religious beliefs at all.

In his study, the dying patients for whom religion was an inconstant emotional crutch seemed to be more anxious. The same findings seem to apply to children. When a dying child has a secure belief in a warm, benevolent God, he seems to continue to be a source of strength and comfort when the child is dying. When the youngster saw God only as someone or something with whom he was threatened in the past in an inconsistent fashion—"if you do not behave yourself, God will punish you"—death is more likely to appear as another threat or another punishment from a vindictive, insensitive deity. The grade school child who has comfortable religious beliefs can see God as the good father and the good teacher, up there somewhere, and the child finds this belief comforting. The preschool child believes religiously in what the parents say, and if they tell him that he will be "safe in Jesus' breast," the child will believe and be happier. He will believe that "Jesus loves me, this I know."

The youngster who has had a rich religious upbringing based on love and understanding will still maintain these basic religious beliefs as a source of comfort and strength, even when he is dying. He may feel angry and resentful at what God has dealt out to him, but this will be anger at a God who really knows best in the long run.

The clergyman must be aware of the significance of religion for each dying child, for he can only help the child at the level the child can use (Cappon, 1959; Nolfi, 1967; Cassem, 1969). The minister should acknowledge his own feelings when he approaches the dying child or the mourning family. Like any other member of the treatment team, he is apt to be deeply disturbed by this youngster who is suffering and who is about to die. He may find that he deals with a youngster in a ritualized, formal manner and uses his ritual as a way to keep a distance from this disturbing child. The minister may joke and laugh as he tends to the child so that he can deny to himself his own sadness or discomfort. Many ministers are made anxious when a dying child expresses anger towards this God who is allowing him to die, and some clergymen try to stop this expression of resentment. However, they should appreciate that the child is more liable to be angry towards those here on earth—the priest, the treatment team and the family—when he cannot express the anger he really feels towards God. Many members of the treatment team and many clergymen could learn from the words of a seventeen-year-old dying adolescent, "If God is as understanding and as powerful as they say he is, he can understand and put up with my anger, for I am mad enough to explode! If God is too weak to tolerate my anger or too stupid to understand, then he is not God!" Clergymen, too, must believe in their God when they are treating the child who is dying. God is certainly strong and understanding enough to take the anger of any dying child or any member of the treatment team.

In the same fashion, physicians, like any other member of the treatment team, deal not only with the painful reality that the child is dying but also with their own reactions to death. The way they respond to this young person who is about to die depends largely on their own personal maturity, emotional understanding and age. Like other young adults, the young doctor and the young nurse are more likely to refuse to accept the possibility of death as a solution to any situation. For young adults, death is something that is to be fought with any means possible. As he struggles against the approach of death in his patients, the young physician is liable to exhaust the child by his efforts; he may even hasten death by the multiplicity of his treatment procedures and by the intensity of his investigations. The young doctor, the young nurse, the young priest, the young parent—all must realize that they are reacting to death with the normal rage of the young adult. They cannot work out this age-specific rage on a young child who is dying.

In the middle years, most people intellectually accept the prospect of death more easily. They realize that dying comes to everyone at some time and in some fashion. Death is now considered to be an interesting experience that can be contemplated statistically or read about in the news media. People of this age recognize that death does occur, of course, and will occur to them sometime, and in this more intellectualized fashion, the middle-aged members of the treatment team deal with the dying child by intellectually accepting what is going on while they try to deny the personal impact. The middle-aged physician is frequently a very competent technician. He knows from years of experience the correct diagnostic and treatment approaches. He has learned the correct technical management of the dying patient and the mourning family. Because the middle-aged doctor is more apt to reduce this very difficult problem to the level of an intellectual endeavor, the staff member of this age may be relatively insensitive to the feelings of his patients or their families. He is more liable to say the correct things at the wrong time. He is prone to make a theoretically appropriate comment when it is realistically and emotionally inappropriate. If he does not carefully monitor how he deals with the family, he will be strong and stern when he should be warm and secure. When the sorrowing parents ask him questions, he is apt to answer with detailed and correct intellectual information when in reality these parents wish a minimum of words and a maximum of comfort. In middle age, treatment team members should be aware that they are more likely to keep themselves emotionally distant from the problems of dying by overintellectualizing the situation. If they are sensitive to this natural tendency at their age, they will be able to be more helpful to the patient who is dying and to his family, who are grieving.

As people get older, they are more likely to accept the reality of personal death with more comfort, and they do not struggle quite as much about this eventuality. They start to make funeral plans for themselves. They prepare wills. In providing treatment and care, elderly staff members must be aware that other treatment team members may not be as comfortable as they are about the possibility of death. Some younger parents and staff members will be personally distressed by the seemingly easy acceptance of approaching death by a senior staff member. If a parent is told, "Your child is better off now," by a kindly, elderly physician after the child has died, the parent is likely to feel deeply insulted or misunderstood. The experienced physician may have wished to be comforting, but he will have provoked anger. When the older physician recognizes that a child is dying, he is likely to be more ready to discontinue treatment procedures so that the youngster dies comfortably. The parents and the younger members of the treatment team are prone to take this treatment stoppage as a form of abandonment. They are likely to protest that the child has only one life to live and that everything should be done to maintain life. The younger parent, the younger nurse and the younger doctor do not accept death as easily as the older staff person may. The young physician is apt to be bothered and annoyed at what he feels to be the lack of care shown by his older colleague who does not battle death on every front and with every weapon. Age may certainly bring an easier acceptance of death, but the elderly doctor must understand that this acceptance comes easier to the aged than to the young.

No matter how the child, the adolescent or the adult responds, no matter whether this be the patient, the parents or a member of the treatment team, each human being has the need to deny some of the deeper uncertainties of death—the possibility of not being, the uncontrolled death agony, the unpredictability of the illness. Every person reacts to death by denying some of the more disturbing aspects of dying. This denial is necessary to allow people to continue. Everyone needs to escape in some fashion from the more frightening or uncertain aspects of death. Physicians, parents, nurses, friends—everyone is likely to be uneasy in some fashion about telling the dying patient that death is approaching because denial then becomes harder to maintain. If the doctor tells the patient that the patient is dying, the physician and the patient share this common awareness of death from that time on. Whenever they look at each other, they cannot avoid thinking death and feeling death. The only way they can escape these feelings is by keeping away from each other. When a doctor prefers not to tell the patient that he is dying, he may be concealing this information not only for the sake of the patient but also for the doctor's own comfort, if he has the responsibility of continuing to treat the patient. When both the parents and the dying child know that death is drawing nearer, it becomes much more difficult for everyone to be emotionally superficial.

The parents and the child, at this time when life is ebbing, have an opportunity for the closest understanding and deepest sharing. They share also at this time a mutual awareness of human frailty, and this can be frightening, very frightening. The doctor who allows himself to tell the patient, child or adult, that death is near leaves himself open to not only the most meaningful but also the most disturbing relationship any professional can have with another human being—the companionship that comes when two people travel together up to the gates of death.

No human being can understand the total meaning of death.
No man can cope emotionally with the full significance of death.
We who deal with death and dying in any aspect must appreciate
and respect the humanity of each of us. We must understand the
burden placed on every individual. We must share the task. The
reality of death has to be faced and should be shared. Death can be
understood as far as the human mind is capable. As man gains an
even greater understanding of death, he reaches for the finite
appreciation of man himself. As Socrates said 2,600 years ago:

> No one knows with regard to death whether it is not really the greatest
> blessing that can happen to a man; but people dread it as though they
> were certain that it is the greatest evil. This ignorance, which thinks
> that it knows what it does not, must surely be ignorance most culpable.
>
> Plato, the *Apology*

Chapter 7

CONCLUSION

In dealing with the dying child, everyone shares a common humanity and must work together. If the doctor can learn how to manage the dying child, he will have reached the heights of his profession, regardless of whether he practices in the most specialized academic center or in the most impoverished slum. The parent who is a good parent to a dying child will learn the deepest meaning of human love and sorrow. The child who lives through the process of dying in the care and the understanding of a dedicated treatment team and a loving family will come to appreciate even more the fullest meaning of life itself.

Death raises many anxieties and uncertainties in the minds of men. The particular genius and strength of mankind comes from the human ability to go on in spite of fears, to grow in the face of dangers and to dream rather than despair. If anyone who lives and works with a child cannot face honestly and deal comfortably with a child who is dying, that person will not only deprive the child of part of the youngster's birthright in living but will also cheapen his own existence and demean his own humanity. The care of the dying not only comforts and gladdens a child who is fatally ill but also ennobles and enriches those who live on.

The care of the young patient who is dying poses the family and the caring professionals with one of the greatest management tasks. The same task offers to these people one of the richest experiences that life can give.

BIBLIOGRAPHY

Abrams, R.D.: The patient with cancer—his changing pattern of communication. *N Engl J Med, 274:*317-22, 1966.

Adams, M.A.: A hospital play program: Helping children with serious illness. *Am J Orthopsychiatry, 46:*416-24, 1976.

Adsett, C.A., and Bruhn, J.G.: Short-term group psychotherapy for post-myocardial infarction patients and their wives. *Can Med Assoc J, 99:*577-84, 1968.

Aldrich, C.K.: The dying patient's grief. *JAMA, 184:*329-31, 1963.

Alexander, I.E. and Alderstein, A.M.: Affective responses to the concept of death in a population of children and early adolescents. *J Genet Psychol, 93:*167-77, 1958.

Anthony, S.: *The Child's Discovery of Death.* New York, Harcourt, Brace, 1940.

Aring, C.D.: Intimations of mortality. *Ann Intern Med, 69:*137-52, 1968.

Bauer, H.: Death and dying: A service focus for school mental health services. *J Clin Child Psychol, 5:*52-4, 1976.

Beigler, J.S.: Anxiety as an aid in the prognostication of impending death. *Arch Neurol Psychiatr, 77:*171-7, 1957.

Benjamin, P.Y.: Psychological problems following recovery from acute life-threatening illness. *Am J Orthopsychiatry, 48:*284-90, 1978.

Bierman, H.R.: Parent participation program in pediatric oncology. *J Chronic Dis, 3:*632-9, 1956.

Blauner, R.: Death and social structure. *Psychiatry, 29:*378-94, 1966.

Bozeman, M.F., Orbach, C.E., and Sutherland, A.M.: Psychological impact of cancer and its treatment. III. The adaptation of mothers to the threatened loss of their children through leukemia: Part I. *Cancer, 8:*1-19, 1955.

Bugen, L.A.: Human grief: A model for prediction and intervention. *Am J Orthopsychiatry, 47:*196-206, 1977.

Bulger, R.: The dying patient and his doctor. *Harvard Med Alum Bull, 34:*23, 1960.

Cappon, D.: The dying. *Psychiat Quart, 33:*466-89, 1959.

Caprio, F.S.: A study of some psychological reactions during prepubescence to the idea of death. *Psychiatr Quart, 24:*495-505, 1950.

Cassem, N.H., Wishnie, H.A., and Hackett, T.P.: How coronary patients respond to last rites. *Postgrad Med, 45:*147-52, 1969.

Chodoff, P.: Adjustment to disability. *J Chronic Dis, 9:*653-70, 1959.

Clayton, P., Desmarais, L., and Winokur, G.: A study of normal bereavement. *Am J Psychiatry, 125:*168-78, 1968.

Craig, Y.: The bereavement of parents and their search for meaning. *Br J Social Wk, 7:*41-54, 1977.

Drotar, D., and Ganofsky, M.A.: Mental health intervention with children and adolescents with end-stage renal disease. *Int J Psychiatry Med, 7:*179-92, 1977.

Druss, R.G., and Kornfeld, D.S.: The survivors of cardiac arrest. *JAMA, 201:*291-6, 1967.

Duff, R.S., and Campbell, A.G.M.: On deciding the care of severely handicapped or dying persons: With particular reference to infants. *Pediatrics, 57:*487-93, 1976.

Easson, W.M.: Care of the young patient who is dying. *JAMA, 205:*203-7, 1968.

Eissler, K.R.: *The Psychiatrist and the Dying Patient.* New York, Intl Univs Pr, 1955.

Eliot, T.D.: The bereaved family. *Ann Amer Acad Polit Soc Sciences, 160:*184-90, 1932.

Evans, A.E.: If a child must die. *N Engl J Med, 278:*138-42, 1968.

Feifel, H. (Ed.): *The Meaning of Death.* New York, McGraw-Hill, 1959.

Freud, S.: [Thoughts for the times on war and death]. In Strachey, J. (Ed. and trans.): *The Standard Edition of the Complete Psychological Works of Sigmund Freud* (Vol. 14). London, Hogarth Press, 1957. (Originally published, 1915).

Friedman, S.B., Chodoff, P., Mason, J.W., and Hamburg, D.A.: Behavioral observations on parents anticipating the death of a child. *Pediatrics, 32:*610-25, 1963.

Furman, R.A.: Death and the young child: Some preliminary considerations. *Psychoanal Study Child, 19:*321-33, 1964.

Furman, R.A.: Death of a six-year-old's mother during his analysis. *Psychoanal Study Child, 19:*377-97, 1964.

Garfield, C.A.: Elements of psychosocial oncology: Doctor-patient relationships in terminal illness. In Garfield, C.A. (Ed.): *Psycho-social Care of the Dying Patient.* New York, McGraw-Hill, 1978.

Gartley, W., and Bernasconi, M.: The concept of death in children. *J Genet Psychol, 110:*71-85, 1967.

Glaser, B.G., and Strauss, A.L.: *Awareness of Dying.* Chicago, Aldine, 1965.

Glaser, B.G., and Strauss, A.L.: *Time for Dying.* Chicago, Aldine, 1968.

Golburgh, S.J., Rotman, C.B., Snibbe, J.R., and Ondrack, J.W.: Attitudes of college students toward personal death. *Adolescence, 2*(6):211-30, 1967.

Green, M.: Care of the child with a long-term, life-threatening illness. *Pediatrics, 39:*441-5, 1967.

Green, M., and Solnit, A.: Reactions to the threatened loss of a child: A vulnerable child syndrome. *Pediatrics, 34:*58-66, 1964.

Greene, W.A.,Jr,: Role of a vicarious object in the adaptation to object loss. *Psychosom Med, 20:*344-50, 1958.

Greene, W.A.,Jr. and Miller, M.: Psychological factors and reticulo-endothelial disease. *Psychosom Med, 20:*124-44, 1958.

Grotjahn, M.: Ego identity and the fear of death and dying. *J Hillside Hosp, 9:* 147-55, 1960.

Gunther, J.: *Death Be Not Proud.* New York, Harper and Brothers, 1949.

Gyulay, J.: *The Dying Child.* New York, McGraw-Hill, 1978.

Hackett, T.P., and Weisman, A.D.: The treatment of the dying. *Curr Psychiatr Ther, 2:*121-6, 1962.

Hamburg, D.A., Hamburg, B., and de Goza, S.: Adaptive problems and mechanisms in severely burned patients. *Psychiatry, 16:*1-20, 1953.

Hamovitch, M.B.: *The Parent and the Fatally Ill Child.* Los Angeles, Delmar, 1964.

Hankoff, L.D.: Adolescence and the crisis of dying. *Adolescence, 10(39):*373-89, 1975.

Hinton, J.M.: The physical and mental distress of the dying. *Q J Med, 32:*1-22, 1963.

Hinton, J.M.: Facing death. *J Psychosom Res, 10:*22-8, 1966.

Hoerr, S.O.: Thoughts on what to tell the patient with cancer. *Cleve Clin Q, 30:* 11-16, 1963.

Hoffman, I., and Futterman, E.H.: Coping with waiting: Psychiatric intervention and study in the waiting room of a pediatric oncology clinic. *Compr Psychiatry, 12:*67-81, 1971.

Howard, J.D.: Fear of death. *J Indiana State Med Assoc, 54:* 1773-9, 1961.

Howell, D.A.: A child dies. *J Pediatr Surg, 1:*2-7, 1966.

Hudson, R.P.: Death, dying, and the zealous phase. *Ann Intern Med, 88:*696-702, 1978.

Joseph, F.: Transference and counter transference in the case of a dying patient. *Psychoanal Rev, 49:*21-34, 1962.

Kalish, R.A.: Death and bereavement: A bibliography. *J Hum Relat, 13:*118-41, 1965.

Kalish, R.A.: A continuum of subjectively perceived death. *Gerontologist, 6:* 73-6, 1966a.

Kalish, R.A.: Social distance and the dying. *Commun Ment Health J, 2:*152-5, 1966b.

Kastenbaum, R.: The realm of death: An emerging area in psychological research. *J Hum Relat, 13:*538-52, 1965.

Keeler, W.R.: Children's reactions to the death of a parent. In Hoch, P.H., and Zubin, J. (Eds.): *Depression.* New York, Grune & Stratton, 1954.

Kennell, J.H., Slyter, H., and Klaus, M.H.: The mourning response of parents to the death of a newborn infant. *N Engl J Med, 283:*344-9, 1970.

Klingberg, G.: The distinction between living and not living among 7-10-year-old children, with some remarks concerning the so-called animism controversy. *J Genet Psychol, 90:*227-38, 1957.

Kneisl, C.R.: Thoughtful care for the dying. *Am J Nurs, 68:*550-3, 1968.

Knudson, A.G., and Natterson, J.M.: Participation of parents in the hospital care of fatally ill children. *Pediatrics, 26:*482-90, 1960.

Koocher, G.P., O'Malley, J.E., Foster, D., and Gogan, J.L.: Death anxiety in normal children and adolescents. *Psychiatr Clin* (Basel), 9:220-9, 1976.

Kubler-Ross, E.: *On Death and Dying.* New York, Macmillan, 1969. '

Langsley, D.G.: Psychology of a doomed family. *Am J Psychother, 15:*531-8, 1961.

LePontois, J.: Adolescents with sickle-cell anemia deal with life and death. *Soc Work Health Care, 1:*71-80, 1975.

LeShan, L.: A basic psychological orientation apparently associated with malignant disease. *Psychiat Quart, 35:*314-30, 1961.

LeShan, L., and LeShan, E.: Psychotherapy and the patient with a limited life span. *Psychiatry, 24:*318-23, 1961.

LeShan, L., and Worthington, R.E.: Some psychological correlates of neoplastic disease. *J Clin Exper Psychopath, 16:*281-8, 1955.

Lester, D.: Experimental and correlational studies of the fear of death. *Psychol Bull, 67:*27-36, 1967.

Lieberman, M.A.: Psychological correlates of impending death. *J Gerontol, 20:* 181-90, 1965.

Lieberman, S.: Nineteen cases of morbid grief. *Br J Psychiatry, 132:*159-63, 1978.

Lifton, R.J.: On death and death symbolism: The Hiroshima disaster. *Psychiatry, 27:*191-210, 1964.

Limerick, L., and Downham, M.A.P.S.: Support for families bereaved by cot death: Joint voluntary and professional view. *Br Med J, 1:*1527-9, 1978.

Lindemann, E.: Symptomatology and management of acute grief. *Am J Psychiatry, 101:*141-8, 1944.

Lourie, R.S.: The pediatrician and the handling of terminal illness. *Pediatrics, 32:*477-9, 1963.

Maddison, D., and Walker, W.L.: Factors affecting the outcome of conjugal bereavement. *Br J Psychiatry, 113:*1057-67, 1967.

Marshall, J.: Helping the grief stricken. *Postgrad Med, 45:*138-43, 1969.

Martin, H.L., Lawrie, J.H., and Wilkinson, A.W.: The family of the fatally burned child. *Lancet, 2:*628-9, 1968.

Maurer, A.: The child's knowledge of non-existence. *J Exist Psychiat, 2:*193-212, 1961.

Maurer, A.: Adolescent attitudes toward death. *J Genet Psychol, 105:*75-90, 1964.

Menig-Peterson, C., and McCabe, A.: Children talk about death. *Omega, 8:*305-17, 1978.

Middleton, W.G.: Some reactions toward death among college students. *J Abnorm Soc Psychol, 31:*165-73, 1936.

Morrissey, J.R.: Children's adaptation to fatal illness. *Soc Work, 8:*81-8, 1963.

Murphy, G.K.: Sudden death in adolescence. *Pediatrics, 61:*206-10, 1978.

Natterson, J.M., and Knudson, A.G.: Observations concerning fear of death in fatally ill children and their mothers. *Psychosom Med, 22:*456-65, 1960.

Nolfi, M.W.: Families in grief. *Soc Work, 12:*40-6, 1967.

Noyes, R.: The dying patient. *Dis Nerv Syst, 28:*790-7, 1967.

Oken, D.: What to tell cancer patients. *JAMA, 175:*1120-8, 1961.

Orbach, C.E., Sutherland, A.M., and Bozeman, M.F.: Psychological impact of cancer and its treatment. III. The adaptation of mothers to the threatened loss of their children through leukemia. Part II. *Cancer, 8:*20-33, 1955.

Raphael, B.: Preventive intervention with the recently bereaved. *Arch Gen Psychiatry, 34:*1450-4, 1977.

Richmond, J.B., and Waisman, H.A.: Psychological aspects of management of children with malignant diseases. *Am J Dis Child, 89:*42-7, 1955.

Rosner, A.A.: Mourning before the fact. *J Am Psychoanal Assoc, 10:*564-70, 1962.

Schilder, P., and Wechsler, D.: The attitudes of children toward death. *J Genet Psychol, 45:*406-51, 1934.

Shands, H.C., Finesinger, J.E., Cobb, S., and Abrams, R.D.: Psychological mechanisms in patients with cancer. *Cancer, 4:*1159-70, 1951.

Shneidman, E.S.: Suicide, sleep and death. *J Consult Psychol, 28:*95-106, 1964.

Shoor, M., and Speed, M.H.: Delinquency as a manifestation of the mourning process. *Psychiat Quart, 37:*540-58, 1963.

Siggins, L.D.: Mourning: A critical survey of the literature. *Int J Psychoanal, 47:*14-25, 1966.

Solnit, A.J., and Green, M.: Psychological considerations in the management of deaths on pediatric hospital services. *Pediatrics, 24:*106-12, 1959.

Solnit, A.J., and Green, M.: The pediatric management of the dying child: Part II. The child's reaction to the fear of dying. In Solnit, A.J. and Provence, S.A. (Eds.): *Modern Perspectives in Child Development.* New York, Intl Univs Press, 1963.

Spinetta, J.J., Rigler, D., and Karon, M.: Personal space as a measure of a dying child's sense of isolation. *J Consult Clin Psychol, 42:*751-6, 1974.

Stedeford, A.: Psychotherapy of the dying patient. *Br J Psychiatry, 135:*7-14, 1979.

Stehbens, J.A., and Lascari, A.D.: Psychological follow-up of families with childhood leukemia. *J Clin Psychol, 30:*394-7, 1974.

Stokes, A.: A game that must be lost. *Int J Psychoanal, 41:*70-6, 1960.

Sudnow, D.: *Passing On: The Social Organization of Dying.* Englewood Cliffs, N.J., Prentice-Hall, 1967.

Sugar, M.: Normal adolescent mourning. *Am J Psychother, 22:*258-69, 1968.

Thomas, L.: Notes of a biology-watcher: The long habit. *N Engl J Med, 286:*825-6, 1972.

Tietz, W., Kahlstrom, E., and Cardiff, M.: Relationship of psychopathology to death in asthmatic adolescents. *J Asthma Res, 12:*199-206, 1975.

Tisza, V.B.: Management of the parents of the chronically ill child. *Am J Orthopsychiatry, 32:*53-9, 1962.

Wahl, C.W.: The fear of death. *Bull Menninger Clin, 22:*214-23, 1958.

Weisman, A.D., and Hackett, T.P.: Predeliction to death. *Psychosom Med, 23:*232-56, 1961.

Weisskopf, S., and Binder, J.L.: Grieving medical students: Educational and clinical considerations. *Compr Psychiatry, 17:*623-30, 1976.

INDEX

113